Postmodern

Paolo Portoghesi

Postmodern

The Architecture of the Postindustrial Society

RIZZOLI
NEW YORK

First published in the United States of
America in 1983 by
RIZZOLI INTERNATIONAL PUBLICATIONS, INC.
712 Fifth Avenue, New York, New York 10019

Translated into English by Dr. Ellen Shapiro

Design
F. G. Confalonieri
Editor
Gail Swerling
Cover illustration
Paolo Portoghesi, Giampaolo Ercolani,
Giovanna Massobrio:
headquarters of the Local Health
Department, Vallo di Diano, 1980-1981

Library of Congress Cataloging in
Publication Data
Portoghesi, Paolo.
  Postmodern.
  The Architecture of the
  Postindustrial Society.

  Translation of: Postmodern.
  1. Architecture, Postmodern.   2. Architecture,
  Modern 20th century.   I. Title.
NA682.P67P67513 1983   724.9'1   82-42857
ISBN 0-8478-0472-0 (pbk.)

This volume was originally published
in Italian in 1982 by Electa Editrice, Milan, Italy

Printed in Italy

Contents

This book is intended as an optimistic chronicle of the events of the past few years in international architecture. The language of Postmodernism — whether or not this word, coined to describe it, finds favor — has spread throughout the world. It has brought into the domain of the contemporary city an imaginary and humanistic component, and put into circulation fragments and methods of the great historical tradition of the Western world that seemed filed away forever, and incompatible with the technological and theoretical conquests of our world. A new force and a new degree of freedom have entered the world of the architect, where for decades a creative stagnation and an extraordinary indolence had rendered the heredity of the Modern Movement inoperative.

The central theme of this book is the image of the Strada Novissima, the first street in the world to run from Venice to Paris and across the ocean to San Francisco, in the mythical West of the United States, where the new postindustrial civilization has developed new models most rapidly. The Strada Novissima is a symbol of a reinterpretation of the Postmodern that brings Europe and America closer; it recomposes, around the theme of the city to be reformed and reimagined, the deep unity of a debate that has upset the precarious balance of architectural culture.

In view of this small revolution that has not abandoned but rather developed the heredity of the Modern Movement, and preserved its strong core of rationality, the label Postmodern, which some protagonists have criticized and refuted, already appears to be an instrument that has seen its day, even if it is still useful from a didactic point of view. The real problem confronting the new generations does not involve finding a label to classify the present and future. The question involves, rather, a turning to a "refound architecture," with no adjectives or formulas, capable of confronting the great themes of postindustrial society.

What is the Postmodern?

"A spectre is roaming through Europe: the Postmodern." A columnist from *Le Monde* gave this title to an article on the most passion-stirring event to occur in the world of culture in the past several years. This phenomenon exploded in America at the end of the last decade, but its roots are especially deep in Europe, where it has found the most fertile ground for theoretical debate.

But what exactly is the Postmodern? Is it possible to give a single definition to such a paradoxical and irritating word? I feel that it is indeed possible. But we must first stop thinking of it as a label designating homogeneous and convergent things. Its usefulness lies, rather, in its having allowed us temporarily to put together and compare different things arising from a common dissatisfaction with that group of equally heterogeneous things called modernity. To put it another way, the Postmodern is a refusal, a rupture, a renouncement, much more than a simple change of direction. To define it poetically, we could borrow the celebrated verses of Montale: "Do not ask us for the key that cannot open... Only this we can tell you today, what we are *not*, and what we *do not* want." And exactly what many of us do not want anymore today is the antiquated Modern, that set of formulas which, in the second decade of this century, acquired the rigidity and clarity of a sort of statute in which general laws are collected that must be obeyed. This statute has never come up for discussion again, even though taste has changed more than once since then. Its main article was precisely an annihilation of tradition, the obligation toward renewal, the theology of the new, and difference as an autonomous value.

This perverse guarantee of perpetual renewal has given modernity the appearance of an elusive shadow, difficult to contend with because of its readiness to assume ever-changing forms and strategies. But in the end, a sense of uneasiness upset even the certainties of the Modern: the discomfort of men of culture when evaluating its products. Sixty years comprise a man's life, and just as a man of this age looks back (and just as the others tend to judge him), the trial against the Modern has been outlined as a physiological necessity, as an unpostponable goal for the new generations, at least since 1968. Therefore, a trial against the Modern and its consequences, but not only this; the Postmodern is a rebellion originating in the realization that in the past sixty years everything has changed in the world of social relationships and production; that industry has undergone radical transformations, and the energy crisis has once more uncovered problems that had been thought to be solved for some time.

The statute of modernity had been custom-made for a society in which the revolution of information that has profoundly shaken all the structures of our world had not yet occurred. Before a Postmodern culture, there previously existed a "postmodern condition," the product of "postindustrial" society. It was inevitable that sooner or later this creeping, underground revolution would end up changing the direction of artistic research. What was less foreseeable was that instead of developing in the futurist-mechanical sense, in the "2000" style, as many had imagined, art steered its course toward Ithaca. It made its way toward the recovery of certain aspects of tradition, and reopened the discussion, the impassible embankment erected by the avant-garde between present and past, and went back to mix the waters with creative results. This recovery of memory, after the forced amnesia of a half century, is manifest in customs, dress (folk, casual and the various revivals), in the mass diffusion of an interest in history and its products, in the ever vaster need for contemplative experiences and contact with nature that seemed antithetical to the civilization of machines.

Architecture was one of the first disciplines to go into crisis when faced with the new needs and desires of postmodern society. The reason for this precociousness is simple. Given its direct incidence on daily life, architecture could not elude the practical verification of its users. Modern architecture has thus been judged by its natural product: the modern city, the suburbs without quality, the urban environment devoid of collective values that has become an asphalt jungle and a dormitory; the loss of local character, of the connection with the place: the terrible homologation that has made the outskirts of the cities of the whole world similar to one another, and whose inhabitants have a hard time recognizing an identity of their own.

The architects of the new generations have made the city, the mechanisms of the production and reproduction of the city, their preferred field of study. They have discovered that the perpetual invention of and search for the new at all costs, the breaking off of environmental equilibria, perspective decomposition, abstract volumetric play, and all the ingredients of modern architectural

8 cuisine were equally toxic to the physiological regimen of urban growth. They have discovered that the imitation of types is more important than linguistic invention. They also realize that it is once again necessary to learn modesty and the knowledge of rules and canons produced over centuries of experiences and errors, that the character of a place is a patrimony to use and not to mindlessly squander. A kind of new renaissance is thus being outlined which intends to recover certain aspects of the past, not to interrupt history, but to arrest its paralysis. And whoever objects that we are in a time of economic and moral crisis hardly fit for a renaissance should be reminded that Brunelleschi's and Leonardo's times were just as dark.

As always, when change is desired, the Postmoderns have also been the target of the arrows of the new conservatives, of those guardians of modernity at any cost, who refuse to relinquish their privileges and power. Unable to refute the radical criticisms of the tradition of the new, they speak of an incomplete project of modernity that must be continued; they pretend to ignore the fact that in order to really change the essential premises of the modern project, and not its last consequences, must be debated once more. And they refuse to admit that continuity with the great tradition of modern art lies today more in the courage to break with the past (which in this case is precisely what was modern yesterday), than in keeping its surviving traces on ice.

In Italy, the harshest and most subtle attack came from the old exponents of the '63 group, which twenty years ago raised the banner of the neo-avant-garde and experimentalism. Precursors of the Postmodern in many marginal aspects of research (the use of the historical quotation, the new-antique corruption, the semiological and linguistic approach), they refuse the products of this new attitude without even analyzing them, making a handy image of these products in order to destroy them with the old weapon of irony. An old system already used once by the enemies of the Modern when it deserved the name. History repeats itself, even if there will always be those who confuse it with a straight line. That postmodern theses have deep roots in the present human condition is confirmed today in the document on architecture issued by the Polish union Solidarity. This text accuses the modern city of being the product of an alliance between bureaucracy and totalitarianism, and singles out the great error of modern architecture in the break of historical continuity. Solidarity's words should be meditated upon, especially by those who have confused a great movement of collective consciousness with a passing fashion.

A New Renaissance

"Zoroaster wants to lose nothing of humanity's past, and wants to throw everything into the crucible."

Nietzsche

During the last decade, the adjective postmodern has made a journey of varying success through the humanistic disciplines. Used systematically for the first time in 1971 by Ihab Hassan in relation to literature, it then made its way into the social sciences, into semiology and philosophy. In architecture, the adjective postmodern found fertile cultural ground, priming a process which started out from criticism and historiography, and finally became the unifying label of a series of trends, theoretical propositions and concrete experiences.

It is worth our while today to reflect upon the unforeseeable fortune of this word in architecure, in order to try to clear up many misunderstandings, and to establish just how useful it can be in relating parallel phenomena taking place in very different areas. In the field of architecture, the term has been used to designate a plurality of tendencies directed toward an escape from the crisis of the Modern Movement with a radical refusal of its logic of development. In the last several decades, this development had led to a chaotic labyrinth, or to the anachronistic attempt to restore the orthodoxy of the golden age of functionalism; the age, of course, of the Bauhaus and C.I.A.M.

The Postmodern has signalled, therefore, the way out of a movement that had for some time stopped "moving ahead," that had transformed itself into a gaudy bazaar of inventions motivated only by personal ambition and by the alibi of technological experimentation. The critics who first put into focus the vast and contradictory phenomenon of an exit from orthodoxy tried to control it by putting it into traditional categories. They also tried to simplify it and make it more comprehensible; but in the end, the neutrality of a word like postmodern is tantamount to an absurd definition based on difference more than on identity. With regard to didactic simplification, the same critics finally surrendered to pluralism and complexity.

Charles Jencks, the most able of the announcers of this new show, proposed that its specificity can in fact be grasped, since it is the product of architects particularly mindful of the aspects of architecture understood as a language, as a means of communication. "A Postmodern building is, if a short definition is needed, one which speaks on at least two levels at once: to other architects and a concerned minority who care about specifically architectural meanings, and to the public at large, or the local inhabitants, who care about other issues concerned with comfort, traditional building and a way of life. Thus Postmodern architecture looks hybrid and, if a visual definition is needed, rather like the front of a classical Greek temple. The latter is a geometric architecture of elegantly fluted columns below, and a riotous billboard of struggling giants above, a pediment painted in deep reds and blues. The architects can read the implicit metaphors and subtle meanings of the column drums, whereas the public can respond to the explicit metaphors and messages of the sculptors. Of course everyone responds somewhat to both codes of meaning, as they do in a Postmodern building, but certainly with different intensity and understanding, and it is this discontinuity in taste cultures which creates both the theoretical base and 'dual-coding' of Postmodernism." (From Charles Jencks, *The Language of Post-Modern Architecture*, London, Academy Editions, 1981.)

This definition certainly covers the unifying aspect of many of the most significant works realized in the last decade which have overcome the ideological crisis of the Modern Movement. It fails, however, to satisfy the historical need of relating the shift carried out by architectural culture to the profound changes in society, and risks confining the phenomenon to an area completely within the private realm of the architect, therefore remaining more a psychological than an historico-critical definition. It is more correct, in my view, to try to get to the specificity of the phenomenon by revealing the substantial differences with modernity, from which it wishes to distinguish itself, in what are its most typical aspects. And since modernity coincides in Western architectural culture with the progressive rigorous detachment from everything traditional, it should be pointed out that, in the field of architecture, the postmodern means that explicit, conscious abolition of the dam carefully built around the pure language elaborated *in vitro* on the basis of the rationalist statute. This language is put into contact again with the universe of the architectural debate, with the entire historical series of its past experiences, with no more distinctions between the periods before or after the first industrial revolution. With the barrier torn down, old and new waters have mixed together. The resulting product is before our eyes, paradoxical and ambiguous but vital, a preparatory moment of something different that can only be imagined: reintegration in architecture of a vast quantity of values, layers, semitones, which the homologation of the International Style had unpardonably dispersed.

The return of architecture to the womb of its history has just begun, but the proportions of this operation are quite different from those which orthodox critics suppose. This reversion to history would always be a laboratory experiment if it were not also the most convincing answer given thus far by architectural culture to the profound transformations of society and culture, to the growth of a "postmodern condition" following from the development of post-industrial society. To convince ourselves, a synthetic review of the historical symptoms of this condition should suffice.

The Age of Information

No technical revolution has thus far produced such great and lasting transformations as the quantification and elaboration of information, made possible by the new electronic technology. Our age has seen the world of the machine, with its working systems and its rhythms, miss the impact of novelty. It has watched a new artificial universe move ahead, composed of wires and circuits, which resemble more organic material than something really mechanical. Information and communication have therefore become terms of comparison with which to redefine and reinterpret the role of all disciplines. And at that moment when the semiotic aspect of architecture and that of the transmission of information, along with its productive and stylistic aspects, was put into focus, it was inevitable that the constrictive and utopian character of the revolution which took place beginning with the twenties, with the worldwide diffusion of the paradigms of the avant-garde, would be evident. In fact, renouncing the systems of conventions through which it had developed uninterruptedly, since the ancient world (the structural principle of the order, base, column, capital, trabeation, and so on), architecture had lost its specificity and had become, on the one hand, an autonomous figurative art, on the same level as painting, or, on the other hand, had reduced itself to pure material production.

Architecture, instead, seen in the area of the different civilization of man, reveals a much more complex nature and role. It is an instrument of the production and transmission of communicative models, which have for a particular society a value analogous to that of laws and other civil institutions, models whose roots lie in the appropriation and transformation of the places of the earth, and which have for centuries played the part of confirming and developing the identity of places (of cities) and of communities.

The result of the discovery of the sudden impoverishment produced in architecture by the adoption of technologies and morphologies separated from places and traditions has been the reemergence of architectonic archetypes as precious instruments of communication. These archetypes are elementary institutions of the language and practice of architecture that live on in the daily life and collective memory of man. These differ greatly depending on the places where we live and where our spatial experiences were formed. The Postmodern in architecture can therefore be read overall as a reemergence of archetypes, or as a reintegration of architectonic conventions, and thus as a premise to the creation of an *architecture of communication*, an architecture of the image for a civilization of the image.

The Fall of Centered Systems

Another aspect of the postmodern condition is the progressive dismantling of the bases of the critical theory of bourgeois society. The sharp polarity of social classes, faith in the redeeming capabilities of the socialization of the means of production, and the analogy of the intricate processes of industrial society in capitalist and socialist countries have placed a profoundly changed reality on guard against the sterility of the dogmatisms and the incapability to explore, with the old tools of consecrated and sclerotic theories.

It should not surprise us that, together with the much more serious and proven ideological scaffolding, even the Modern Movement is in crisis: a variable and undefined container, within which quite different and often divergent phenomena were placed. This was an attempt to construct a linear function of architectural progress, in regard to which it would be possible at all times to distinguish good from evil, decree annexations and expulsions as in a political party. The Modern Movement proposed to change society for the better, avoiding (according to Le

12 Corbusier) the revolution, or carrying it out, as the Russian Constructivists believed. Among its great tasks, the most important was that of teaching man to become modern, to change his way of life according to a model capable of avoiding waste. Today, this undertaking hardly seems valid for a colonialist program, while the real problem is one of understanding what postmodern man wants, and how he lives. He is not an animal to be programmed in a laboratory, but an already existing species which has almost reached maturity, while architects were still trying to realize their obsolete project of modernity.

The great intellectual work done in the past twenty years on the concept and structures of power has put another drifting mine beneath the fragile and suspect structure of the Modern Movement. Separating the idea of power from the relationships of work and property "in which," as Alain Touraine has written, "it seemed to be totally incarnated," even the role of the architectural avant-gardes has been able to be analyzed in different terms, recognizing its responsibilities and inadequacies, and putting in crisis the theory that stripped them of responsibility. They attributed all blame to the "design of capital."

The history of architecture of the past thirty years could, therefore, be written as the history of a "way out" of the Modern Movement according to a direction already experimented by the masters in the last years of their lives, at the beginning of the fifties.

The crisis of theoretical legitimation, which Jean François Lyotard calls the "scarce credibility of the great Récits," and the fact that today we must confront the problem of the meaning "without having the possibility of responding with the hope of the emancipation of Mankind, as in the school of the Enlightenment, of the Spirit, as in the school of German Idealism, or of the Proletariat, by means of the establishment of a transparent society," has unhinged the fundamental principles of architectural modernity, consisting of a series of equations which have never been verified except through insignificant small samples. These are the equations: useful=beautiful, structural truth=esthetic prestige, and the dogmatic assertions of the functionalist statute: "form follows function," "architecture must coincide with construction," "ornament is crime," and so on. The truth of architecture as a simple coincidence of appearance and substance contradicts what is greatest and most lasting among the architectural institutions, from the Greek temple to the cathedral; and even what the Modern Movement built under the banner of truth often has its worth in an "appearance" that has little to do with constructive truth. The great moral tale that hoped to grasp the human aspect of architecture, theorizing its function and "sincerity," by this time has the distant prestige of a fable.

In place of faith in the great centered designs, and the anxious pursuits of salvation, the postmodern condition is gradually substituting the concreteness of small circumstantiated struggles with its precise objectives capable of having a great effect because they change systems of relations.

The Crisis of Resources and the City-Country Relationship

The postmodern condition has put into crisis even that discipline that the Modern Movement had placed beside architecture, as a theoretical guarantee of its socialization: city planning understood as the science of territorial transformations. From the time when city planning, abandoning the tradition of nineteenth-century urban rhetoric, had become that strange mixture of ineffectual sociological analyses and implacable zoning, the city seemed to have lost the very principle of its reproduction, growing from the addition of fatty or cancerous tissue, lacking essential urban features, as in the great peripheral areas.

The most obvious symptom of the change in direction of architectural research was a return to the study of the city as a complex phenomenon in which building typologies play a role comparable to that of institutions, and profoundly condition the production and change of the urban face. The analytical study of the city has skipped over the functionalist logic of the building block, reproposing instead the theme of the continuity of the urban fabric, and of the fundamental importance of enclosed spaces, actual component cells of the urban environment. The study of collective behavior divided the criterion of the dismemberment of the urban body into its monofunctioning parts, the standard which informs ideal cities, proposed as models by the masters of modern architecture.

The energy crisis, on the other hand, and the crisis of the governability of the great metropolitan administrations has focused once again on the problem of the alternatives to the indefinite growth of the large cities, and on the necessity of correcting the relationship of exploitation still characterizing the city in relation to small centers and the region. The great myth of the double equation, city=progress, development=well-being has given way to the theory of limit and of controlled development. With regard to a postmodern urbanism, an institutional reformism is beginning to be considered that would give new competitive strength to smaller centers through federative initiatives (in Italy, a process of this kind is going on in the Vallo di Diano, under the aegis of Socialist administrators). Ecological problems and the energy crisis have led to the self-criticism of the acritical propensity toward the new technologies that have substituted old ones, often with no advantage whatsoever for the life span of the product, the absorption of manpower and esthetic quality. A change of direction is inevitable if we do not want to further aggravate economic and social problems. To realize the importance of these programs, it is sufficient to reflect upon the fact that the energy consumption of a plastic panel is twenty times that needed for the construction of a brick wall of the same area, or that the progressive disappearance of certain trades because of the abandonment of certain techniques would render us, for a lack of skilled workers, unable to restore historic monuments and ancient cities, whose integral preservation seems to have been, at least on paper, one of the great cultural conquests of our time.

The truth is that the postmodern condition has reversed the theoretical scaffolding of so-called modernity. Those who are amazed that, among the most apparent results of the new culture in its infancy, there is also a certain superficial feeling for a "return to the antique," seem to forget that in every serious mixture, the artificial order of chronology is one of the first structures to be discussed and then dismissed. Just as grandchildren often resemble their grandparents, and certain features of the family reappear after centuries, the world now emerging is searching freely in memory, because it knows how to find its own "difference" in the removed repetition and utilization of the entire past. Recently in Japan, sailboats have been built whose sails are maneuvered not by hundred of sailors, but by complicated and extremely fast electronic devices. These ships, equipped also with conventional engines, allow for a great saving in fuel. Postmodern architecture, whose naïve manifestations of a precocious childhood we see today, will probably resemble these ships that have brought the imaginary even into the world of the machine.

The End of Prohibition

John Blatteau: *Architectural self-portrait for the exhibition "The Presence of the Past," 1980.*

14

The Biennale Exhibition "The Presence of the Past"
In July 1980 the Venice Biennale inaugurated its first international architecture show entitled "The Presence of the Past." Thanks to the spectacular Strada Novissima realized expressly for that occasion, the exhibition has become almost the symbol of Postmodernism. Here is how the exhibition was presented in the catalogue under the banner of "The End of Prohibition."

Rather than attempt a systematic, neutral review of architectural "quality" wherever it can be found in the complex phenomenology of present architecture in the world — a notarial task requiring measuring instruments discredited by the crisis of the discipline — we preferred to choose a theme, and hence a "movement." With this last word, we do not intend an organized tendency endowed with an orthodoxy of its own, but rather a phenomenon coming into being, to be listened to and understood more than to force and direct, where problems, discomforts, and even the discoveries and desires of a certain time are explained; "our time," with regard to which — as Walter Benjamin wrote about his own experiences — it is important, without deluding oneself, "to state one's opinion without reservations."

With the title of the exhibition "The Presence of the Past," we hope to take hold of a phenomenon which has its symptoms in the fifties, in the courageous turn of direction in the research of the masters of modern architecture, but has carried on, with a slow and arduous rhythm, transformed only in the past few years into a radical and definitive effort. This phenomenon is the direct comparison, with no defences or inhibitions, with architecture as one of man's permanent institutions, and therefore with the history of architecture as a unitary system where the experiences of the relationship between man and earth, the operative and cognitive conquests of a defined sector of human work converge.

The ideology of modern architecture thought it had rid itself of this whole of languages, human institutions, and conventions with a stroke of the eraser, proclaiming its obsolescence in the new times. But it had actually continued to live in the memory of man, renewing itself constantly since it was fed by the "presence of the past," by messages that continue to originate from that set of tangible things called historical heritage as a whole, and from a new viewpoint produced by the contents of the "human condition."

The return of architecture to the womb of history and its recycling in new syntactic contexts of traditional forms is one of the systems that has produced a profound "difference" in a series of works and projects in the past few years understood by some critics in the ambiguous but efficacious category of Postmodern.

The word modern, originally designating continual change, has undergone a process of sclerosis in identifying itself with a style, contaminated by the stasis of an unproductive situation.

Paradoxically, it has become the symbol of an abstract power to be fought and overturned.

In choosing a title different from Postmodern, this exhibition proposes a clarification. In fact, in choosing a sphere both vaster and at the same time more restricted within a great area of phenomena still only temporarily classified, it intends to point to the changes of the specific disciplining of linguistic exigencies rather than to the psychological attitude with which the forms, whatever they are, are used. A "postmodern condition" exists, created by the rapid structural change of our civilization. It is easy to foresee that other, more precise and appropriate philosophical diagnoses will be added to the first ones. This new condition can be explained in architecture in two ways, one totally ideological, concentrating on what has changed inside us, and therefore on the inevitably different way we perform the same acts we performed before. The architect lives this presence observing himself, describing himself, noting that the collapse of illusions modifies his sense of work, gives new meaning to the old operations of the avant-garde, creates around these operations a halo of silence, or a magic play of mirrors which satisfies both the desire for play and the need for tragedy.

The other way is that of looking beyond oneself and observing that architects are not the only "priests" who change the reality of architecture, but everyone else, and it is not only they who work in this sector of human endeavor, but it is also they who suffer, use and consume it. It is enough to accept this principle to realize that the axe invented by historians to divide ancient from modern architecture never existed in the minds of the users of architecture, but only in the minds and intentions of the "employees." Recognizing the "postmodern condition" in this second way, through architecture and not through ideology, means both denying any definitive break in the

BIENNALE DI VENEZIA

THE PRESENCE OF THE PAST

IT IS AGAIN POSSIBLE TO
LEARN FROM TRADITION AND
TO CONNECT ONE'S WORK WITH
THE FINE AND BEAUTIFUL
WORKS OF THE PAST. JOHN BLATTEAU

PER ME QUOD
ERIT QUE FUIT
QUE EST QUE
PATET

Hommage à Vitruve, Perrault,
Le Noir Le Romain, Blère,
Henry, Hector Guimard, Loos,
A. Perret, Asplund et Le Corbusier.

DAVID BIGELMAN   JEAN PIERRE FEUGAS   BERNARD HUET   BERNARD LE ROY   SERGE SANTELLI   **TAU**

T.A.U. Group (David Bigelman, Jean Pierre
Feugas, Bernard Huet, Bernard Le Roy,
Serge Santelli): *Architectural self-portrait
for the exhibition "The Presence of the
Past," 1980.*

Fabio Reinhart, Bruno Reichlin:
*Architectural self-portrait for the exhibition
"The Presence of the Past," 1980.*

17

concreteness of architectural institutions and recovering that character — rightly emphasized by Robert Venturi — of "expert in conventions," through which it is possible to "communicate" not verbal messages, but architectural thoughts, thereby socializing intellectual work without outdated populist aspirations. The choices made and the inclusion and exclusion in the group of architects invited begin from this basic hypothesis, which privileges transformations of language and the abandonment of Modernist orthodoxy, and singles out in the "relationship with history" the central knot which permits the establishment of the boundaries of a movement and the perception of a "before" and an "after" regarding something precise that happened in architecture.

This does not mean that the choice of the architects invited to participate corresponds rigorously to a homogeneous design. The advisory committee of the section, comprised of Nino Dardi, Rosario Giuffré, Giuseppe Mazzariol, Udo Kultermann and Robert Stern, decided to involve critics like Vincent Scully, Christian Norberg-Schulz, Charles Jencks and Kenneth Frampton in the organization of the exhibition, in order to guarantee a range of different and at times diverging interpretations of the theme proposed by the director of the section. These interpretations can be compared to one another in the preparatory debate and clearly communicated to the visitors to the "Presence of the Past" through special exhibitions.

Kenneth Frampton's progressive detachment and eventual withdrawal of his participation in the choices for the exhibition (due among other things to his proposal to include Rem Koolhaas in the twenty planners of the "Strada Novissima") indicates how the resulting picture, even in its plurality, is not so neutral that it does not produce disagreements and incompatibility. Originally perplexed by the excessive openness ("I see this Biennale as a pluralist-cum-postmodernist manifestation; I am not at all sure that I subscribe to this position, and I think I will have to keep my distance from it"), Frampton then cultivated a clearer refusal of the comprehensive viewpoint of the exhibition, and even decided to exclude his prepared text from the catalogue. ("The critical position it adopts is so extremely opposed to all that could be summed up under the category Postmodernist, that I realized it would be absurd for me to advance the essay in this context.")

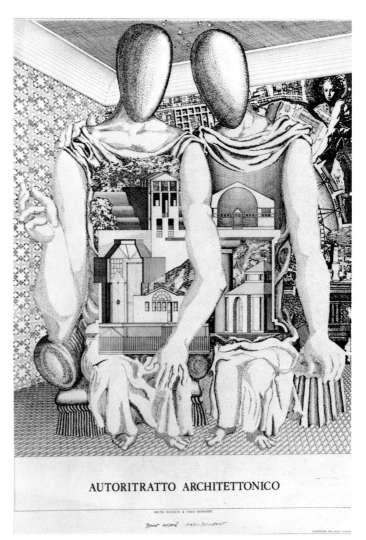

AUTORITRATTO ARCHITETTONICO

Six images shot from below of the Strada Novissima at the Corderie of the Arsenal, Venice, 1980.

18 This exhibition really attempts to cast doubt on the first aggregations made in function of a category like Postmodern, all the more useful the more it extends beyond the boundaries of architecture, trying to form a relationship with what is happening in converging directions in the most diverse disciplines, and has made the magic work ricochet from philosophy magazines to literary, economic and political magazines, insofar as it is possible to reconstruct history.

Getting rid of a category because of its ambiguity, or because "others" whose company we do not want have taken shelter under it (and perhaps they try to elbow out those preceding them) is understandable. But it does not help us to understand or clarify such a complex and hardly controllable reality. The reign of architectural magazines and their power groups has in the past few years become a sounding board for a strongly guided radical turning point.

But by now, the undulatory motion is too strong to be brought back to order and channeled into preconstituted designs. For years we have opted for a "criticism of listening" whose objective is change, and not the forecast or the illusory planning of some consultory "final solution," and less than ever the sterile game of verifying the correspondence between what happens and the great central schemes of philosophy and history. In the sphere of a strategy of listening, the exhibition on "The Presence of the Past" will help as many people as possible to have a better understanding of the fact that several important things have changed even in architecture, and that the "subjects" of architecture are not only the architects. It will serve — and in this the direct interlocutor is Italian culture — to announce the end of that "prohibition" which for years has repressed the instinct to use everyone who agrees to communicate with us as materials for the present, without preconceived discrimination, to involve memory and imagination with the maximum effectiveness, the projection into the future and the desire for environmental quality.

In Italy, official criticism, with its judicial methods, is still ready to see the dangers of involution, infantile regression, the return to the academy wherever research leads to the recognition of the fundamental role of memory in the process of the communication of architecture. The prefix "neo" applicable to any "style," ancient or modern, has served to brand with infamy and to break off at

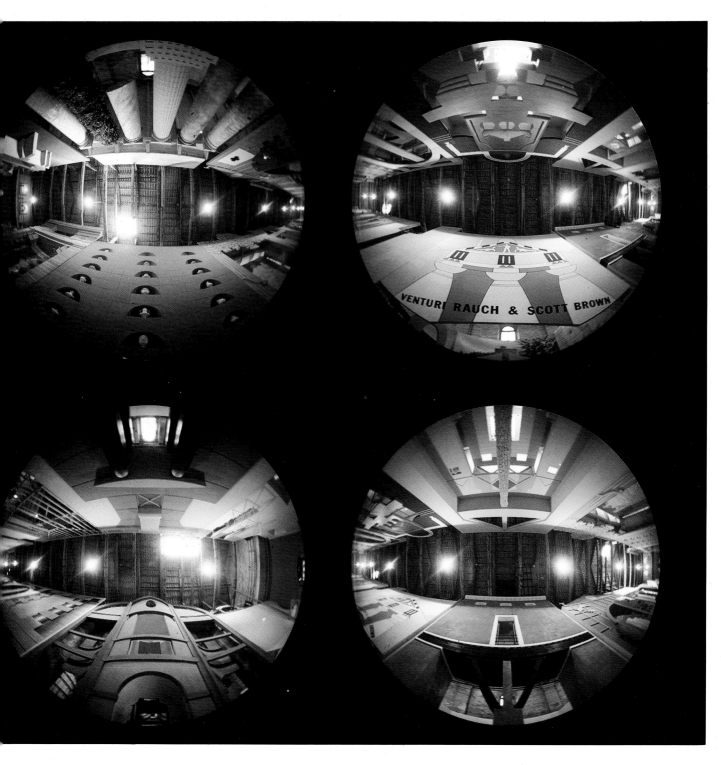

Charles Jencks, Christian Norberg-Schulz:
*Critics' Hall at the exhibition "The
Presence of the Past," Venice, 1980. The
big metaphorical pencil is by Charles
Jencks, the diorama along the walls by
Christian Norberg-Schulz.*

20   birth all attempts at opposition to the conformism of a
culture that oscillates, like a mad pendulum, between
arbitrary invention and the passive acceptance of
technological mythologies. The priests of the Modern
Movement continue to recite their litanies on the basis of
untenable identifications between classicism and authoritarian regimes, between eclecticism and creative
sterility, as if thirty years of research had not definitively
rid the historian's desk of the opposing pairs of concepts
dear to old high-school teachers, and of the mechanical
connections between political content and artistic forms.
Even so, the barrier of prejudices circulating with such
patient continuity is no longer effective. The young no
longer believe in the totems or taboos of this withered
religion. By now, the excommunications and invectives,
the slanderous tricks of judicial criticism remind us of the
police tricks of the prohibitionists. They bring to mind
the famous Izzy Einstein Chew who, disguised as a
longshoreman, arrested an Italian who had carefully
hidden tiny bottles of liquor in his cash register; or,
another time, entering the Half Past Nine Club in New
York playing the part of a rich poultry merchant, he
found a large quantity of illegal beverages in a huge
stuffed bear. By now, there are so many stuffed bears
around that the work of critic-policemen is difficult, and
prohibition seems over forever. As we predicted, its end
has carried with it many intoxications and exaggerations,
but also a certain type of enthusiasm that will perhaps
make us remember these years (and the Venice exhibition) as full of vital ferment where irony and nostalgia,
disenchantment and "sympathy for things" are mixed. In
a certain sense, these are the years of "refound time," to
use a Proustian image.
The negation of the past, or rather the rigid morphological separation between present and past desired by the
Modern Movement, was a typical defense mechanism, to
use the Freudian term for negation. "The cathartic illusion," wrote Marcello Pignatelli, "of freeing ourselves
from all dross and obstacles, of cutting the knots of
conditioning and guilt, of waking up different tomorrow,
destroying yesterday's house full of unbearable
memories, really means projecting the internal conflict
onto a magical act, in the impossibility of elaborating on
it."
The reproposed "presence of the past" is neither simply
ironic, nor, least of all, purely unnecessary and con-

Façade of the Strada Novissima at the Corderie of the Arsenal, Venice, 1980. This page, from left to right and from top to bottom: façades by Hans Hollein, Joseph Paul Kleihues, Robert Venturi, Franco Purini and Laura Thermes.
Opposite page: interior of the façade by the Taller de Arquitectura of Ricardo Bofill.

sumerist. It contains a great deal of truth because it realizes its impotence in elaborating a real psychological conflict. The possibility of confronting and resolving the problem of replanning the city depends on overcoming this conflict. This is seen in the unresolved contradiction between historic centers and periphery, between the space of meaning and quality (that of the ancient city) and the space of quantity and absence of meaning (that of the periphery). Closed in the ghetto of the ancient city, memory has become inoperative, a factor of separation and privilege. Circulating once again in the present city beyond the fences erected to defend its alleged purity, memory can help us leave our impotence behind, and exchange the magical act that once deluded us into exorcizing the past and building a new world without roots, for the lucid and rational act of the reappropriation of the forbidden fruit.

We can already predict the reactions to the exhibition. There will be an attempt to proclaim the consumption of the Postmodern category, or an attempt to classify the recycling of historical forms as reproductions of the Surrealist avant-garde, or the Beaux-Arts method. And there will certainly be someone who, making a connection between what is going on now and the symptoms of the fifties, from New Sensualism to Decorativism and neo-Liberty, will predict the marginality of an elitist movement seemingly unable to upset the consolidated establishment of official architecture indentured to the International Style. As always, whoever is forced "out of bounds" in his field of research by something he had not foreseen, tries for a "removal" as a last defense, and expects his revenge from time and from the mistakes of others. But the objective of the exhibition is so ephemeral and untriumphal, that these objections or prophecies only confirm its timeliness.

If this is an elite phenomenon, then why not verify its capacities for enlargement, involvement, contagion? If its mythologies are far from the real problems of the growth and reorganization of the territory, then why not verify it by observing, studying, trying to understand if instead it contains indirect indications for the solution of these problems? If everything we can observe in this exhibition were simply the cyclical reflowering of a nostalgia that has already demonstrated its ephemeral character many times, then why not realize with our own eyes if the diagnosis is correct, if those emerging elements are really

missing that allow us to consider this culture of the image, this approach to the past, by now qualitatively incomparable to the symptoms and anticipations advanced? The strategy of listening, the critical willingness to attentively consider the results of any new regrouping of works, even the least approved and authorized, eliminates even the fears and accusations regarding inclusions and exclusions. The choice was made collectively and is therefore inevitably compromising. It has the merit, though, of being a dialogical choice, and so has the advantage of bringing together things born in different climates and sensibilities. It also helps us to see intellectual work as a symptom of a common lymph circulating not only in the ordered network of canals that our minds can imagine, but also in the labyrinthine circulatory system of the ideas of a new human condition, experienced before it is interpreted and made conscious.

Other objections will be raised concerning the forced coexistence of at least three tendencies with different declared programs. I allude to European neo-rationalism, whose ramified structure descends from the teaching of Rossi and from what is called "La Tendenza," to the semiological poetics of the first "Five," to urban classicism flowing into the anti-industrial resistance which constitutes a partial branching out within the tendency, to the radical eclecticism theorized by Charles Jencks. The opinions of the other directors of the exhibition concerning these classificatory hypotheses are revealed in their writings and in their direct participation in the exhibition. We assume full responsibility for temporarily setting aside the categories mentioned, since we feel it more opportune to consider discriminating, not intentions and theories, but architectural facts, morphological choices: that is, the way of thinking *with* architecture and not *about* architecture. The consequence is certainly the heterogeneity of the contents and principles underlying the forms. But it was much more important for us to propose the demythologization of a method that, putting forms and ideologies together and considering them indissolubly tied, ended up in a ridiculous court of history, condemning structures, methods, and collective patrimonies, comparable to those conquests of science whose only fault is having been adopted by people with not very recommendable police records. It seems strange, but in a world which has become more tolerant and understanding of deviance, and where no one would

*Views of the Strada Novissima at the
Corderie of the Arsenal, Venice, 1980.*

26 dream of disdaining Caravaggio's work because the artist was violent, or the work of Michelangelo for his particular inclinations, symmetry is still branded and considered synonymous with homosexuality, and classicism as something irremediably contaminated by the use made of it by certain political regimes.

The declarations of poetics in this catalogue are an extraordinary illustration of the variability of intentions that can inspire intellectual work. And given the singular adherence to the proposed theme of the exhibition, these declarations also illustrate the different attitudes toward the past marking the personalities and groups identifiable on the basis of geographic and cultural areas. We are really interested in declaring the richness of the motivations and thoughts that animate a great common effort, that of linking old and new, of contaminating memory and the present, of gradually focusing a set of contrasting methods, a patrimony of experiences which, summed up and compared, already make possible the identification of a long road of collective research. This writer holds it opportune to set aside the sectarian attitude which would lead to setting the protagonists of the front singled out by the exhibition against one another. The reopening of boundaries that delimited the language of uncontaminated geometry and separated it from the forest of symbols and connections of historic memory has at times been interpreted, in theoretical propositions, as the reopening of a one-way street toward other firm certainties, toward an orthodoxy of an opposite, but no less risky, sign. A new classicism as a moment of the "eternal return," or an architecture of illuministic reason adapt as little to present reality as the dogmas of the functionalist statute and the myths of technology. No less illusory is the romantic return to the healthy virtues of the pioneers in a world which the energy crisis ought to make move backwards. The past whose presence we claim is not a golden age to be recuperated. It is not Greece as the "childhood of the world" which Marx talked about, ascertaining the universality, duration and exemplariness of certain aspects of European tradition. The past with its "presence," that can today contribute to making us children of our time, is the past of the world. In our field, it is the whole system of architecture with its finite but inexhaustible sum of experiences connected or connectable by a society which has refused a monocentric culture, a main tradition with no competition. Nineteenth-century eclecticism had already recognized this curvilinear horizon that makes us embrace a visual field of 360° and denies us the privilege of a fixed orientation with respect to which everything is measured. But the eclecticism of that time, like old imperialism, proceeded from a sort of natural history of civilization, from a systematic cataloguing of closed repertoires, or from their naïve mixture directed toward the realization of characteristic beauty, or toward assigning styles a value of illusionistic contents in the great history of urban typologies.

The relationship with the history of architecture which the postmodern condition makes possible does not need the eclectic method anymore, because it can count on a form of "disenchantment," on a much greater psychological detachment. The civilization of the quantified image, the civilization of sacred images that knows the barbarities of the new imperialism and its progressive shattering can use the past without being more involved in illusory revivals or in naïve philological operations. History is the "material" of logical and constructive operations, whose only purpose is that of joining the real and the imaginary through communication mechanisms whose effectiveness can be verified; it is material utilizable for the socialization of esthetic experience, since it presents sign systems of great conventional value which make it possible to think and make others think through architecture.

In this sense, architecture can once again be returned to the places and regions of the earth without a return to a racial or religious metaphysic. It can be the means of removal of the old Europocentric system based on the myth of classicism. It can also be the recognition of the relative and partial validity of all conventional systems provided that one accepts belonging to a polycentric network of experiences, all deserving to be heard. Entering postindustrial society, knowledge changes its statute.

The process of "getting informed" which characterized the past few decades symbolizes a new Copernican revolution whose constructive and destructive consequences we are only beginning to understand: the intense and continuous circulation of images and data, the possibility of more and more easily approaching complete statistical knowledge, the resorting to probabilistic methods, which in successive attempts simulate once quite long processes of comparison and elaboration. The acceleration of many processes and the miniaturization of instruments, the use

of models and analytic programs have accelerated the crisis of the great centered systems in the field of epistemology. And it is easy to predict that the same thing will happen in a short time for the methodological patrimony of the human sciences and specific operative techniques. "It can be suggested," Jean François Lyotard wrote, "that the problems of internal communication that the scientific community meets in its work, taking apart and putting back together its languages, are comparable in nature to those of social collectivity when, deprived of the culture of *récits*, it must test communication with itself and interrogate itself about the legitimacy of decisions made in its name."

The collapse of the great summarizing discourses that propose unitary interpretations and programmatic prophecies, (it is the incredibility toward them that qualifies the Postmodern position, according to Lyotard) makes the strategy of listening obligatory, and the intellectuals can regain a specific role in the self-interrogation of real society as regards its desires and objectives.

The architects' interest in history and in the recycling of forms and traditional compositional systems should also be seen in relation to this self-interrogation, to this census of still valid or confirmable conventions, to the restitution of the role of subject to the community of its users, after the long parenthesis of the claim of this role only by the "technicians of form," made legitimate by the theory of the Modern Movement.

Mass culture produces a continuous wave of information and images that reproduce originals, but that also tend to substitute and underrate them, rather than create sacred auras around them. Seeing a purely negative phenomenon in this underrating and quantification of access means simply continuing to use an aristocratic viewpoint and not knowing how to grasp the liberating result and the egalitarian charge of this profanation of the myth. Together with the inhibitions imposed by prohibition, the devotional attitude toward history hidden behind the negation of its real value also collapses. Like the Renaissance, with the reawakening of critical conscience and the birth of philology, it has marked the true definitive separation from the ancient world (to which, paradoxically, it wanted to link up again); thus, the end of prohibition and the recycling of traditional forms marks the definitive separation in architecture from the near past, from the inextricable mixture of Illuminism and Romanticism making up the modern tradition. A decisive step ahead is thus made toward the laicization of the discipline.

It is not the task of this introduction to effect the historic reconstruction of the "movement" which the exhibition attempts to outline with the force of its images, or to establish the role of the protagonists and the quality of their contributions. In organizing the exhibition, we preferred not the place of the critic or historian, but of the architect who "puts into action" his discipline, builds a platform from which to speak first of all with his language. Elsewhere we tried not to make history, but to systematically display some aspects of the movement (cf. Paolo Portoghesi, *After Modern Architecture*, New York, 1982); we would especially like to clarify the objectives and the method that inspired the exhibition of seventy-six architects — a section of "tributes" ideally placed first — comprised of Philip Johnson, Ignazio Gardella and Mario Ridolfi. The organizers intended to complete this section with a show of Carlo Scarpa's drawings, but a hurried and reductive effort was discouraged for reasons of organization, and also because a large retrospective of Scarpa's work will be held in 1982. The choice of Johnson, Gardella and Scarpa is a recognition of their importance in the creative reintegration of historical heredity and repudiation of the binding orthodoxy of the International Style. In Johnson we wanted especially to remember his lucid work of testimony that, after interpreting the concrete result of the Modern Movement in a well-defined practice, was the first at the beginning of the sixties to declare, with no regrets, the sterilization and death of a by now immobilized movement. The proximity of the exhibition dedicated to Ernesto Basile completes the section of the tributes with a reminder of the importance that the revaluation and study of Art Nouveau had in the cultural formation of many architects of the last generation included in the central exhibition. The initial intention to put on other exhibitions dedicated to Josef Hoffman and Bruno Taut next to the Basile show, but later postponed because of organizational difficulties, would have clarified how it is possible to identify a vein of self-criticism of fundamental importance within the modern tradition, and very similar to the present revisionist orientation. Even the first project for the central exhibition included names which are missing from the final cast, cancelled after ample discussion by the consulting committee, whose results were respected by the director

(but not by the directive council, which voted by a majority for the inclusion of two other names in the list of the
twenty architects of the Strada Novissima). I feel it my
duty to mention that initially the following were included
in the twenty names selected for the street project:
Roberto Gabetti and Aimaro d'Isola, Guido Canella,
Ricardo Porro, Hassan Fathy, and in that of the
exhibitors, Piero de Rossi, Uberto Siola, Nicola Pagliara.
The idea of the Strada Novissima with its twenty façades
answers the intention immediately immersed in the preparatory discussions, of insisting on the possibility of its
realization, and of involving the architects invited to the
show in a concrete operation offering the public the
chance for direct tactile and spatial contact with architecture. At first, we thought of suggesting one or two themes
related to the Venetian territory. Among the hypotheses
was that of redesigning the steamboat landings.
The hypothesis of the street was born in December in
Berlin, in the climate of the Christmas festivities, during a
seminar organized by Paul Kleihues in which Carlo
Aymonino and Aldo Rossi participated. After a dutiful
tribute to Schinkel, and near the Alexander Platz, between the echo of the late Behrens and the outlines of the
Stalin-Allée, we discovered a marvellous enclosed amuse-
ment park with a small piazza surrounded by small
stands that imitated façades of houses in temporary materials, the ground floor in true scale and the others in a
scale of 1:2, a paradoxical answer to one of the needs of
the city, a need for closed and inviting space at the center
of one of the crossroads of modern architecture.
The desire to build a "space of the imaginary" in the
center of the exhibition has its immediate result in the
image of that temporary architecture made for play,
animated by the crowd and where, as on a stage, there
was always an inside and an outside, a part for the
employees and another for everyone else. The fair seemed
to be a simple eloquent metaphor for the relationship
between architect and client, mediated by the group of
façades that are also faces, the sign of an identity transferred to an object. In this way, the idea came up for the
street inside La Corderia of the Arsenal, a gallery of
architectural self-portraits made for play, for rediscovering the very serious game of architecture, a game on
which even the quality of our life depends somewhat.
It is not by chance that the Strada Novissima was realized
by the Organization for the Administration of Cinema in
the laboratories of Cinecittà. Since its birth, cinema has
been the factory of the imaginary, and for many generations it was the only possible access to an aspect of life
exorcized from the other sectors of human life. The street
is built in temporary materials using refined artisan
techniques that the world of cinema has miraculously
saved. But what was seen unanimously as an element of
weakness can today be seen instead as an element of
interest and strength. As a temporary and transportable
piece, a machine in the ancient sense, the Strada Novissima links up again with the tradition of temporary urban
furnishings that gave the city a different face, with its
seasons and recurrent or exceptional events. The making
private of urban space, the abolition of the street and the
piazza as places established for meetings and exchanges,
has pushed aside the temporary urban space, reducing it
for the most part to the fanciful illuminations of patronal
feasts. In a city reinterpreted in function of the new
collective needs, the temporary space can reacquire its
importance and become an instrument for the socialization of urban space and the continual creative reinterpretation of its appearance. The experience of the Venetian
Carnival in 1979 administrated by the theater section of
the Biennale directed by Maurizio Scaparro, is one dem-
onstration of this potential for rediscovery, interpreted
also by the great sign of the Teatro del Mondo. Of all
Italian cities, Venice is perhaps the one with the richest
and most significant tradition of temporary space, seen in
the floating machines and in the structures that can be
reassembled in the fair of the "Sensa" and which can be
considered prefigurations of our street.
The result of planning provocation lies completely along
the lines of irony and autobiography, but has a strong
communicative impact: it is a happily scandalous result
that promises to stir up discussions and arguments, and
to involve visitors not in a useless and anachronistic
agreement, but in a critical adhesion, in a reawakening of
a conscious question of the imaginary as an antidote to
urban sterility. Naturally, the exhibition has not produced and does not propose models. It does not intend to
resolve "the problem of housing," but to propose through
graphic evidence the "problem of the city," to affirm the
principle that the problem of housing can be resolved
only through the confrontation of the problems concerning the quality of the urban environment and its symbolic
recodification. Architecture in action was the Teatro del

30 Mondo that Aldo Rossi designed, forcing the impossible scenery of the San Marco basin to reopen a dialogue, interrupted for centuries, in a new way. Architecture in action is the Strada Novissima that reaffirms the centrality of the theme of the street as an instrument for the reintegration of the urban organism. Architecture in action is also the choice of the Arsenal, the splendid space of La Corderia that seems to contain Piranesian space *in nuce*. Realizing the First International Exhibition of Architecture in the Arsenal, and symbolically projecting a piece of the city onto it, the Biennale intends to be a Trojan horse in a desirable restitution to Venice of one of its most vital organs. The military authorities and the Revenue Office have demonstrated far-sightedness and sensibility for the public interest in conceding such a prestigious space for an exhibition. And the city of Venice, allowing for an initial restoration, has crowned this gesture of solidarity toward this new-born sector of the Biennale, making its immediate use possible. Now, the future of the Arsenal acquires a new value and concreteness. Its future destination could open up the narrow spaces of a city that can grow only within itself, and on the other hand, cannot be happy with surviving only for others. This great structure of Venice, which has always been a prohibited space and an unadmired wonder, finally opens its doors to the public. We would like the birth of the architecture section of the Biennale to be identified with this symbolic act.

From "The Presence of the Past. First International Exhibition of Architecture," Venice 1980.

Hopes and Fears

Following the ancient example of the travelling theater, the Strada Novissima, born in the half-light of the Corderie of the Arsenal, in what was for centuries the productive center, the "workshop" of Venice, has been dismantled and has begun a journey that will carry it across the ocean. "Everything that is heavy will become light," wrote Nietzsche, "may everything that is body, dance and everything that is spirit, fly."

For a moment, architecture returns to the condition of the theater, of the stage, and detaches itself from the place that generated it, while its message becomes independent of geographical location. This is a strange paradox for an exhibition that celebrated the return of architecture to the place, to its concrete roots on earth. But it is a significant paradox, since it sprang from a desire to demonstrate the coincidence of both a return and a new departure. The return to the womb of its history, which the new generations have imposed on architecture, coincides in fact with a new journey in a world where sense has lost its stability, forms have lost their univocal character and have acquired a disquieting transparency. Borges says this in his *Arte Poetica*: "They say Ulysses, wearied of wonders,/ wept with love on seeing Ithaca/ humble and green. Art is that Ithaca,/ a green eternity, not wonders./ Art is endless like a river flowing,/ passing, yet remaining, a mirror to the same/ inconstant Heraclitus, who is the same/ and yet another, like the river flowing." (Translation by Anthony Kerrigan, *Jorge Luis Borges*, *A Personal Anthology*, New York, Grove Press, 1967.)

The exhibition dedicated to the "Presence of the Past" gathered together the documents of a new voyage of Ulysses which the architects, by now close to a new *fin de siècle*, have undertaken, "wearied of wonders," tired of perpetually inventing, surprised at having rediscovered through history, through a refound familiarity with their craft, the "green eternity" of Ithaca, the eternal present, the conventions of collective memory that at times deceptively and at other times more concretely permit them to emerge from isolation, to speak once again with architecture in an accessible and direct way to everyone.

The return to Ithaca is also a definitive estrangement, because Ulysses is no longer the same: inconstant like Heraclitus, one and different like the "observed" water of the river, he sees a "different" Ithaca with new eyes that his long experience has filled with images.

The Strada Novissima can thus be considered a street in Ithaca. Its symbolic meaning would be even more exact if it had been a *rio* in Venice, a street of water whose bottom surface is also constantly variable. The incompleteness of the symbol is now replaced by the removal and loss of the fixed reference, of the local identity. And the fact that the first stop is Paris, central city of the West, crossroads of every artistic thought, capital or reference point of avant-gardes, is another symbol that must be interpreted. Even if the objective, or one of the objectives of this exhibition is that of reestablishing the relationship with the place, it does not aspire to an impossible restoration of nationalistic myths, but to a definitive recognition of one of the vital conditions of the culture of our time: the universality of its space and its comparative nature in plurality.

From the very beginning, mobility was one of the objectives of this exhibition. Its transferral, like its expansion or its reduction, was also realized. Born from the convergences of several critical hypotheses, the exhibition does not avoid but rather takes upon itself the contradictions of the architectural debate. It has proven itself to be a "machine for thought," a machine that has pushed its countless commentators to express themselves, to say what they feel about a concept, the concept of "postmodernity," which was excluded from the title of the exhibition in order to avoid disputes about its name. But words, as we know, have a fascination of their own, and for the word postmodern we could repeat what Aragon said of the word modern, that "donne toujours à ses adversaires l'air de courir après leur ombre," (*always gives its opponents the appearance of running after their shadow*) except that in this case, even the shadow is doubled, as in a mirror image, and the pursuit is more difficult and illusory.

The extraordinary attention given to the exhibition and to the Strada Novissima in the international press — together with Aldo Rossi's Teatro del Mondo, intended as its prefiguration — demonstrates the opportunity of having set in motion a machine of this kind to think about and enjoy architecture, the usefulness of extending the debate well beyond the confines of specialized criticism. Rather than call attention to the many enthusiastic responses and the more or less critical adhesions, we would like to recall the anxiety and fear generated by this cultural event, since these responses are fundamental to clearing up the misunderstandings, and for understanding the possible directions of the development of architectural research. We shall, therefore, speak about the "fear of heresy," of the "fear of hegemony," of the "fear of memory," and the "fear of regression."

These four themes are decisive for the future of the most radical and profound attempt at a change in direction that has been taken in the field of architecture in the past sixty years.

The Fear of Heresy

The Modern Movement originated as a great pluralistic program attempting to reify the spirit of the time, the Zeitgeist, catching it in its initial stages in the different cultural realities of the European and American horizons. After thirty years of free experimentation, (Art Nouveau, Protorationalism, Expressionism, the modern classicism of Behrens, the creative eclecticism of Sullivan and Wright) the Modern Movement, beginning in the twenties, tended to translate into a set of constraining rules, into a real orthodoxy, three fundamental dogmas: *the functionalist analysis* as a starting point for architectural research; *the annihilation of the traditional grammar of architecture* with all its differences corresponding to places and civilizations; *the identification between architectural progress and the use of new technologies* understood as potential generators of language. These three dogmas have been criticized and completely removed from the new culture with the stimulus of social and cultural factors typical of postindustrial society. These factors involve everything from informatics to the energy crisis, from the emergence of problems of the Third and Fourth Worlds to the crisis of ideologies and the frightening uglification of the cities. It is no wonder that this inversion of tendencies, which in certain respects has led the conditions of research back to the climate of eclecticism and freedom of the premodern phase, is the object of the most violent attacks by those who, in good faith or not, do not realize how much the world has changed. Under the pretext of curing the world of its ills, they continue to propagandize old formulas whose ineffectiveness has already been extensively demonstrated. Since it tried to focus not on the thousandth extension and deformation of a movement, but on a phenomenon of removal, of a definitive exit, the exhibition seemed sacrilegious, and has caused a visceral and infantile reaction. Since everything removed from truth is false, and everything removed from the eternal is ephemeral, it follows that the Postmodern is false and ephemeral, or rather, a nightmare, and we can already exalt post-Postmodernism.

To those who submit to this thesis, we could answer once again with the words of Zoroaster: "What do these houses mean? A silly child pulled them out of the toybox. But will not another child want to put them back in the box?" The Modern Movement has no more right to eternity than other movements and tendencies that preceded it and will follow it. Art must not be conditioned with the constraints of ideology and the methods of religions. It is important, rather, to check at all times whether any ideological umbrella (the Modern Movement was reduced by its theoreticians to a real umbrella protecting it from all risks) causes its *raison d'être* to go into crisis: its freedom, inseparable from the possibility of becoming the interpreter of the constantly changing "Spirit of the Time." Historical documents demonstrate that at least since the twenties, the Modern Movement has imposed on the entire world an unprecedented levelling (Pasolini would have said "homologation") of the linguistic means of architecture, imposing the destruction of archetypes upon which its system of communication was based, along with the annihilation of its local codes which explained, in the differences in cultures, the differences among men and their collective identity. In exchange for a plunge into the intellectual purity of the language of Euclidean geometry and a parallel ideological recharging, the Modern Movement, in its dogmatic result identified with the functionalist statute, has established a limitless empire, the empire of Esperanto, or better, of aphasia, held together by unprecedented aristocratic rules. In this empire there is an abyss between the masterpieces and anonymous works, where quality is reserved for the select few, capable of attaining absolute originality and cultivating a "personal style" in which the poor quality of the others makes the works of the masters shine all the more. The current defenders of modernist orthodoxy are never concerned with the fact that the international victory in this annihilation of archetypes resulted not only from a fascination with ideology and promises of salvation, but also from the perverse collaboration of the logic of profit and bureaucratization, which saw in the new language the most efficient tool for erasing the problems of the rise in the cost of labor and of the many "superfluities" tied to civic value and representing architecture. They have always waged their battle using moralistic blackmail and emphasizing the noble battles fought (mostly by their predecessors) against academic reaction.

The last line of defense for exorcizing heresy attributes the crisis and failures of the most significant objectives of modernity to insufficient time and, therefore, asks for an appeal, for a delay in retirement. But what arguments do they have — and this is, afterall, the main point — to maintain that they can give an answer to the degradation of the city, using the obsolete instruments of the Modern Movement?

The blame for this degradation is put on *power* in its different forms. But it is difficult not to attribute the role of secular arm to a discipline that has given power all its instruments, furnishing it with extenuating circumstances and theoretical justifications.

The heretical revision carried out by the architects in the Venice and Paris exhibitions based on a structural critique of the modern city and its living conditions, comes before all other ideal incentives. Within this framework, a comparison is justified and useful.

The Fear of Hegemony
The Venice exhibition has stirred up anxiety not only in the public, but also in the participants themselves. On the day before the opening of the show, I saw many creators of the façades of the Strada Novissima wandering around in the half-light of the Corderie, puzzled by their own work and by the work of the others. They seemed anxious, as if involved in a rally that might degenerate into a riot and confuse their good intentions with the bad ones of their companions, some of whom might be armed with Molotov cocktails.

If my impression is accurate, they were concerned most about the degree of memory and about European-American hegemony. The number of architects from the United States, seven out of twenty, seemed insufficient to the supporters of the Postmodern as an American product. Their number seemed excessive to the Europeans, worried about protecting their identity and the autonomy of their research, often out of phase and quite different from that of their colleagues across the ocean.

What sense is there in placing Ungers and Gordon Smith, Venturi and Rossi, Graves and Krier on the same level? These people have often polemicized with one another,

and often have trouble understanding each other. With all due respect for these anxieties, we would like to exhort visitors and protagonists of this new addition of the exhibition in the church of the Salpêtrière to reflect upon the value of diversity, to understand the potential of critical reflection which develops from a comparison of such different solutions, whose only link is that of resorting freely and unashamedly to collective and individual memory.

The Europeans do not all agree on a presumed homogeneity of the Americans, but are here to represent their differences, to call attention to a revision that is still incomplete and hence more open and stimulating. But keeping in mind this typically European geography made up of proud isolation, of indecision and reserve, should we make a critical comparison with the open-mindedness and pragmatism of some of the Americans, willing to experiment every road to the end and to start from the beginning whenever they glimpse a valid alternative?

The title "The Presence of the Past" used in Venice responded perhaps more directly to the American approach, which instinctively underrates the temporal and consequential dimension of history, and sees the past as a closed system, as a synchronic system similar to a repertoire, which it is natural to reach without any constraints except that of the symbolic value of architectural signs. The "Presence de l'Histoire," the title used in Paris, seems to reflect more the European approach to history as a casual connection of events, as an irreversible succession in which everything that happens afterward must be an "overcoming" and therefore give an account of the entire past. But even in this case, comparison is very useful as a critical tool. And although it might sound like a reprimand to those who have evasively forgotten the great page of modern thought, and behave like "resuscitated Giulio Romanos," it makes us think about the great efforts at synthesis of some European civilizations to bring history back into a synchronic system. This was first done by the Greeks, who interpreted ethnic and local traditions as compatible "orders," and established the fertile rules of an eternal present that can be attained without contradictions.

The Small Fear of Memory
The most common worry, outside and inside the stands of the Strada Novissima, was the fear of memory, the bibli-

*Façade by Christian de Portzamparc (left),
and façade by Paolo Portoghesi (right) in
the Paris edition of the exhibition "The
Presence of the Past" in the church of the
hospital La Salpêtrière, 1981.*
*Façade of the Strada Novissima
reassembled in the form of a piazza, Paris,
1981.*

cal fear of stopping too long to look back and being turned into a statue of salt. This is not surprising, since the most vital part of Western culture decreed the annihilation of traditional architectural codes in the twenties. With regard to "recognized" architectural forms endowed with a history and a "name," a tacit agreement of prohibition was reached, sparing only those elements that were sterilized and reappropriated by the science of construction. From then on, if we omit that sort of limbo in which traditionalists of greater or lesser lineage continued to work, from Lutyens to Brasini, the architect abstained rigorously from the prohibited diet, and developed a real complex of inhibition.

The Strada Novissima with its twenty façades (which became twenty-two and twenty-three in the other editions) presents all the possible degrees of the process of reappropriation of memory and the victory over inhibitions inherited from rebel fathers. It is precisely in this wealth of nuances that its greatest value can be seen, not as an impossible model of a street in a real city, but as a street of streets, a route that unites, or at least sums up, twenty possible completely different streets; not all of them are correct, of course, but they are all in some way oriented toward this renewed and uninhibited relationship with history. This is a physiological relationship that finally renders justice to the pathological relationship established by decree and imposed with obstinate rigor. In order to focus on the intensity of the relationship with historical memory, it is necessary to show two parallel and opposite movements from which the meaning and the value of the relationship arise. These two movements are similar to those of an oscillating pendulum; one turned toward the past, the other toward the "removal" of the past, and therefore to its actualization. The instruments used to realize the first movement are the direct quotation, the abstraction of a model, the individualization of an archetype to be evoked. The instruments used for the second movement are simplification, caricatural deformation, the inversion from a positive to a negative form, metaphoric irony, and plastic reinterpretation. In trying to attribute a decisive movement to the second movement, that of "removal," it is easy to single out those architects in the exhibition who have most convincingly hit their mark. But not infrequently, the depth of the probing toward history does not correspond to the success of the "removal." The sequence of the façades has that rare

quality of making us think not only about the styles that characterize the presence of the new masters, but also about the road that still must be taken in order that this reemersion of archetypes really become a cognitive conquest, and not end in a new avant-garde experimentation. In view of what has been said, there was not and could not have been an excess of memory in any of the architects. Even Greenberg's literal quotation, or Gordon Smith's deliberate total recovery of order, take on meaning as demonstrations of the futility of looking for removal, since it is already present in the sensibility of its users, and in the provocatory act of exhumation.

On the other hand, the end of prohibition in architecture is a conquest that brings this discipline into an area of linguistic freedom that all the other artistic disciplines had either conquered without causing scandals, or had never lost so completely. Who would ever dream, for instance, of taking away the patrimony of spoken languages from modern literature, and abolishing all the traditional codes? Who ever berated Saba or Eluard for writing sonnets? And in modern painting, has there not always been a figurative current often fed by the cult of memory, alongside the integralism of constructivism and abstraction? Picasso was allowed to express himself in a plurality of interchangeable languages and to establish a kind of intellectual commerce with history. Le Corbusier, on the other hand, for love of theory, inflicted upon himself a kind of mutilation, refusing his early works, so precious today for understanding his intellectual biography and so convincing in their approach to history. In the area of modern orthodoxy those who more or less consciously continued, like Frank Lloyd Wright, to use decoration and some historical reminiscences, were often mistreated and accused of inclinations toward kitsch. We need not even mention that Stalinist-type trial carried out against J.J.P. Oud for having dared to conceive of the Shell building in The Hague in terms of perspective symmetry.

Those who fear a wave of permissiveness would do well to remember that the ironic use of the quotation and the archaeological artifact as an *objet trouvé* are discoveries of the figurative avant-garde of the twenties that have landed on the island of architecture sixty years late. There is something else in agreement with the vindication of memory, and the linguistic freedom opened up toward the past is only a means behind which a different, more

La Strada Novissima at the Fort Mason Art
Center, San Francisco, 1982.

37

ambitious program is hidden. This program is the hope of giving a lost concreteness back to art, a materialistic and symbolic base through the reemergence of archetypes. Architecture carries the concept of ἀρχή (*arkhè*) inseparably immersed in the word designating it. In Greek mythology the Muses were born from Mnemosyne, to mean that there is no art except that originating from memory, and in some way a repetition. Even the Modern Movement fed unwillingly on memory, and its masters are also prophets of this small revolution we see occurring before our eyes.

But in a world calling for increasing capacity, for control and critical consciousness, it makes sense that today the most sensitive architects prefer the concrete memory of forms, the conscious memory to the denied and unconscious memory, to the hidden and esoteric memory filtered through geometry.

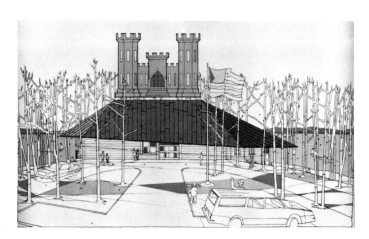

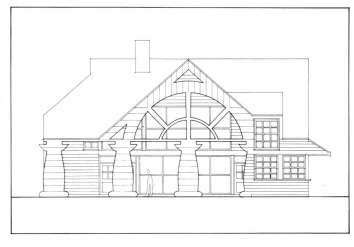

The Small Fear of Regression

The last, but certainly not the least, of the anxieties stirred up by the postmodern wave involves the political sense of its orientations. One of the theoretical matrices of the revisionist direction that we have tried to represent is certainly a tiredness toward the mechanical connection between architecture and politics through ideology, which constituted one of the greatest hopes of modern architecture. Yet, it has proven to be one of its great mistaken aspirations, in whose name innumerable acts of mischief and ridiculous simple-mindedness have been committed.

Historians of architecture who do not overly disdain the scientific method, and who have some taste for the documented verification of their assertions, know that the identification of a repertoire of forms with a political tendency or even with a more general vision of the world of the reaction-progress type, is always vain and mystifying. Between architectural forms and political practice and theory there can exist temporary reciprocal acts of instrumentality, convergences involving material interests, and elective affinities felt sincerely by someone or other in one of the two fields, but not much more. The rest consists of mystifications or news items having little meaning in the long run.

The penalization or exaltation of fashions or style because they are favored by dictators or by great supporters of democracy is part of an amateurish and journalistic

Robert Venturi: *Brant House, Tuckers
Town (Bermuda), 1976–1980.*

tendency that is fortunately disappearing. One of the great merits of the young generations is their important contribution after the events of 1968 to the defeat of the conformism of contents upon which a certain left-wing rhetoric was based which made great use, when required, of the most opportune "philosophy of history."

Farewell, then, and let us hope forever, to the myths of politicized and demagogic architecture, of Socialist and Fascist architecture, and so on.

The tragic facts of Italian architecture during Fascism, when the most diverse architectural tendencies, be they modern, conservative, or modern-conservative, were involved in a contest to see which could declare itself the most Fascist, the most authentically Fascist, should be a lesson to all.

There is a great difference between this and proclaiming that architecture and politics are two extraneous and unconnectable things. There is no doubt that one of the tasks of the new architectural culture is the clarification of the sense of its apparent disengagement.

One of the typical conquests of this new attitude is the reconsideration of *Classicism* outside of ideological disputes as an intensely disciplinary guiding idea that acts and has acted in the most varied linguistic contexts, and still has great critical force.

Classicism is not a style, but a way of looking at architecture as one of man's institutions. It is no longer understood as the art of a perfect and balanced society to be nostalgically evoked, but as a way of thinking about architecture that makes use of certain historical invariants of the collective memory, of the possibility of agreeing by referring to a patrimony of conventions revisted and shared critically by society.

Leaving critical consciousness aside, some worry if this indiscriminating use of the historical memory is in itself a backward attitude, and therefore one which intentionally denies "progress." How can this retrospective attitude escape the risk of relating to and being resonant with reactionary and regressive political attitudes? The answer is simple. Reintegrating historical forms into the repertoire of present architecture, comparing this patrimony to the positive heredity of the Modern Movement, and making these two aspects of the "past" interreact is anything but a traditionalist choice. It is related less than ever to regressive political attitudes. As always in history, the new tendencies have aimed at the objective

40

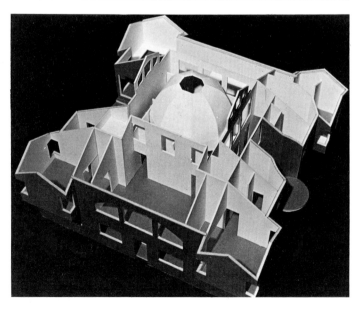

of differentiating themselves from what came before, from the attitude of their fathers and older brothers. Since this attitude had been crystallized in the cult of perpetual renewal at all costs, the differentiation could consist only in opposition to this labor of Sisyphus, proposing a reform of method, a renunciation to a state of research that had become pathological because of the precariousness of its methods and the impossibility of setting up stable means for the verification of personal choices.

The breakdown in the production and reproduction of the city by the culture of the analytic approach has brought about a turning point that obeys not a desire for preservation, but the "instinct of preservation." It proposes a return, but a return to a physiological state that comes after a pathological period in which architecture makes sense only if it is considered as a pure art in the nineteenth-century and Romantic sense, and not as a moment in the productive work of man.

Modern architecture has certainly deposited its masterpieces in the bank of history to be labelled and put in an ideal museum. But next to this quality without quantity, is quantity without quality, the loss of the identity of the built environment, the homologation of cultures, the cultural imperialism of the West and the suicide of weaker cultures faced with the Moloch of technological internationalism. For deciding in favor of a reintegration of archetypes that would bring architecture back to the origin of its nature as a human institution based on conventions, participated in by everyone and transformable only through long collective processes, intensely political aspirations of a return to the craft, of an abandonment of ideology understood as a false conscience, as a cover used by intellectuals to hide their neurosis of a separated body, have had a profound influence on the new generations.

At least in this sense, behind the disengagement — to be interpreted correctly as recognition of the autonomy of architecture — lies an indication of intellectual honesty corresponding to an idea of architecture that is anything but neutral and reactionary, an architecture which may not have the characteristics prescribed by a certain populist participation (the design decided upon by the users, the voting on of technical decisions, and so on). But this architecture is certainly closer to the majority of people than that technocratic architecture which arose from the crisis of the Modern Movement because it con-

Thomas Gordon Smith: *foreshortened view of the Tuscan House and the Laurentian House, Livermore (Ca.), 1979.*

stantly borrows from a common patrimony. It is inalienable and stamped on the minds of everyone through the common experience of historical space, because it makes an appeal to conventions of universal value corresponding not to ideological superstructures, but to permanent characteristics of the perception and appropriation of space.

Think, for example, of the return to symmetry and repetition, perhaps the most considerable and coherent of the mutations going on in the domain of the new architecture. One of the most dogged theorists of modernist theories, Bruno Zevi, has written in his book *The Modern Language of Architecture*, that symmetry is an intolerable cancer and can be compared in a Freudian sense to homosexuality. In this summary process, however, Zevi has let himself be seduced by the silly divagations of a psychoanalyst, instead of interrogating the history of architecture. Had he done this, he would have realized that the symmetry of a building or an environment is the most direct expression of an instinctive tendency toward the identification of man with his product, and with the organization of his vital space. He would also have realized that the prohibition of symmetry corresponds to an attitude as intolerant and authoritarian as the imaginary one he assaults.

It is not by chance that a precise echo of the task of historical reintegreation of the historical patrimony, as a premise of renewal, is to be found in a document of Solidarity, the free Polish union fighting to give Socialism a new democratic face.

"Totalitarianism, the principal feature of 20th century architecture," the document reads, "is not only the result of socio-political systems. Blind faith in progress, the mythology of science and technology, the huge numbers involved in the increasing population, pluralism confused with chaos, all this has created the belief that man himself does not know how he must dwell and live. And that in its place it is up to architecture to know. Nobody has imposed upon architects the idea of utopian needs for typification and prefabrication rather than real needs: nobody has inflicted upon them to neglect the value of temporarily isolating pollution in urban areas instead of neutralizing it at the sources, nor to yield to spatial schemes that divide and separate that which, essentially, forms a unity. Architects are responsible for the present state of Man-Architecture-Environment relations to the

Thomas Gordon Smith: *section of the project for a house in Matthews Street, San Francisco, 1978.*

Thomas Gordon Smith: *project for the Lang House, Carson City (Nev.), 1978.*

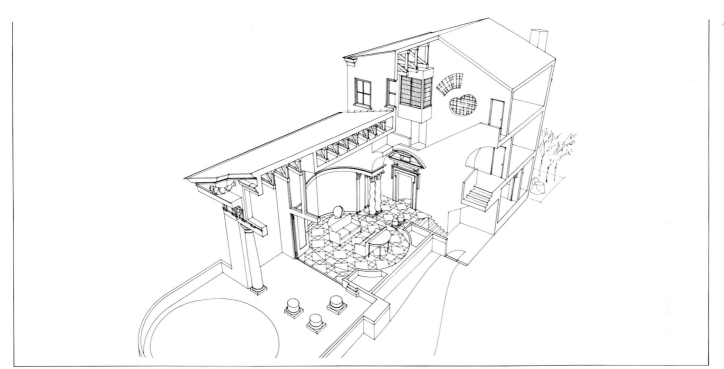

William Turnbull: *Moss House, 1978.*

Robert Mittelstadt: *house in San Francisco, 1980.*

46

measure in which they are engaged in creating these ideas.

The greatest error of architecture, born from the spirit of the Charter of Athens, is the rupture in the continuity of culture. It must not be forgotten that the destruction of the traditional town was done in the name of sublime ideals: the right of man to a brilliant life, to sun, to contact with nature. The heritage of the past has been put into a kind of museum. The architecture of our century opposes ideology to life, projects to reality. Instead of making our profession a task more and more complicated and further removed from reality, an architectural continuity must be recovered which searches for new fundamental architectural ideas such as style, method and dogma."

Solidarity's analysis takes off from the crisis of the city and comes to conclusions no less radical than those that have emerged in the Western world: "The architect is neither the omnipotent master nor the slave of spaciocultural models, universal or local. His proposed role is to interpret them within the framework of the continuity of civilization. Reducing architecture to its utilitarian function is to remove its role as a means of social communication. From the moment the language of models was replaced with the newspeak of towers, bars and *grands ensembles*, the town has become monotonous, illegible and dead for its inhabitants. A town must be built on the basis of elemental housing models, roads and squares."

Solidarity's analysis corresponds exactly to the diagnosis of the new architectural criticism. The fact that this analysis is the outcome of a great experience of struggle only confirms the solid and profound roots of the sociocultural movement that has become clear in architecture, and that goes beyond the traditional confines of the political order.

In this attempt, consisting of rebellion and reintegration, can be seen one of those basic movements arising in the domain of culture that represent, beyond the sclerosis of some traditional political forms, a symptom of the political vitality and spontaneous organization of citizens against power in its most diverse forms.

"Today," Alain Touraine has written, "likewise we live amidst a multiplicity of ruptures and initiatives that certainly do not all relate to the same body, but that contribute very much to the formation of a new cultural field and social movement. We should listen and interpret its

Robert Mittelstadt: *house in San Francisco,*
1980.

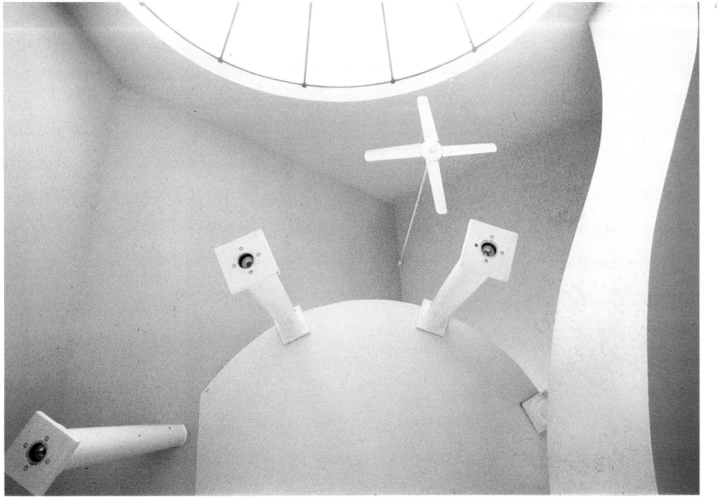

48

call. Conflict, protest, initiative are present everywhere, even if weak and disorderly..."

The international movement that has manifested itself — even in contradictory forms — in the field of architecture, and that proposes as its unitary objective the reintegration of archetypes, is probably one of the great sectorial movements in which several sociologists single out the future of the great struggles for the emancipation of humanity after the fall of illusions about the possibility of giving a definitively "human" face to power.

"With the belief in 'progress,'" in André Gorz's words, "by the development of industry, science and technology, a positivist conception has died which likened the State to Supreme Goodness, and politics to religion and even morals. Even now, we know that there is no 'good' governing of a 'good' State, a 'good' power, and that society will never be 'good' by virtue of its organization but only by reason of the spaces of autonomy, self-organization and voluntary cooperation that it offers to individuals. The beginning of wisdom is in the discovery that contradictions exist in which there are permanent tensions, and that certainly no resolution must be sought; it is reality at its specific and separate levels that must be taken into account and must not be reduced to an 'average.' That necessity is without morals and morals without necessity."

In a future prospect — divested of the great totalizing illusions but not of the tension toward justice — architecture will be able again to assume its ancient role as mediator between man and nature, as guardian of the conventions and experiences characterizing the places of the world in their infinite diversity.

In light of these considerations, the effort made by the latest generations of architects to go consciously beyond the blind alley into which the Modern Movement had led us, appears as an indispensable step ahead. And if it does not resolve the contradictions between architecture and power, it helps to position them in a more advanced way. We can await the "democratization of architecture" not only from the new architecture, and not only from a methodological mutation and reintegration of archetypes; even this small revolution of clerics is shortening the way toward the restitution to the people of the power to choose freely and to contribute to determining the spaces in which they live.

Luciano Patetta: *project for the Diocesan
Museum in the San Eustorgio complex,
Milan, 1980.*

Francesco Cellini: *Alpha houses,
Ciampino, 1972.*

Francesco Cellini, Nicoletta Cosentino,
Claudio d'Amato: *project for the
competition for Les Halles, Paris, 1979.*

Charles Jencks: *Garagia Rotunda, Cape Cod (Ma.), 1976–1977.*

Bruno Reichlin, Fabio Reinhart: *front view of the Sartori house in Riveo (Vallemaggia), 1976-1977.*

Ante Josip von Kostelac: *Malchen House, Germany, 1976.*

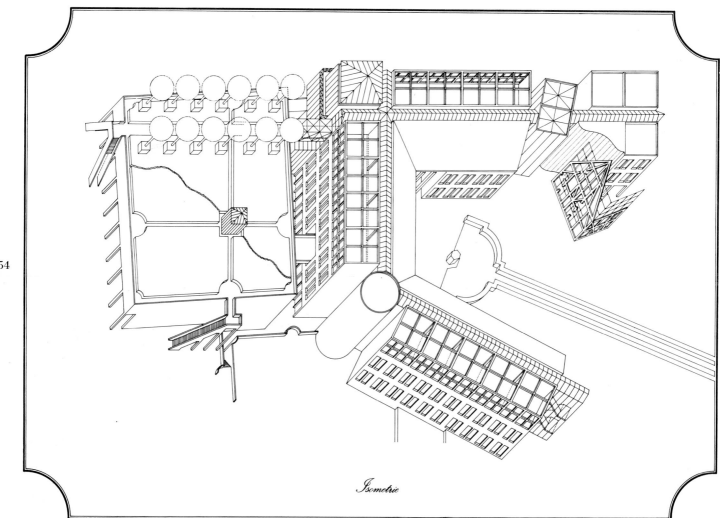

Isometrie

Ante Josip von Kostelac: *competition project for the Rosdorf School, 1977.*

Joseph Paul Kleihues: *museum project, Blankenheim, Germany, 1976–1979, general view.*

Lluis Clotet, Oscar Tusquets: *view of the Belvedere Giorgino, Llofrin, Gerona, Spain, 1972.*

Hans Hollein: *palm-columns in Austrian Travel Agency, Vienna, 1978.*

Jeremy Dixon: *residential units, St. Mark's Road, London, 1979.*

Ines Lamounière, Patrick Devanthery: *project for Fiumicino, 1981.*

56

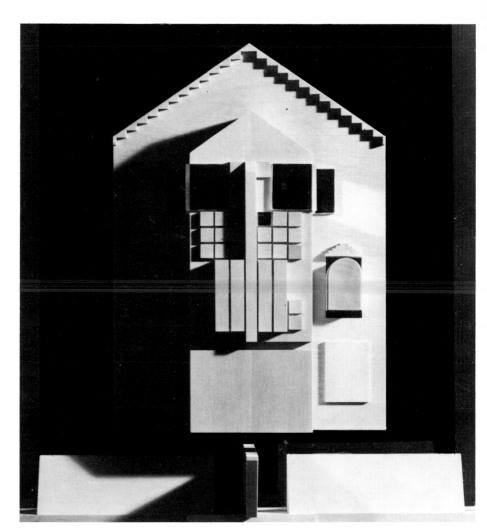

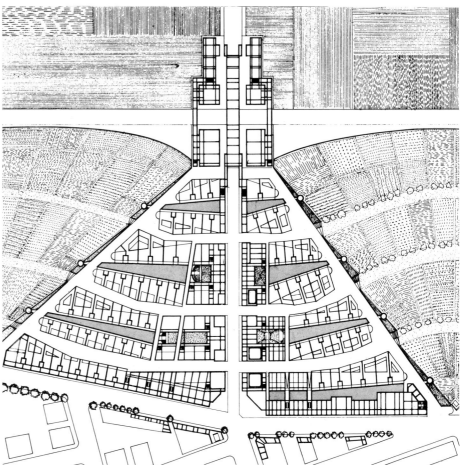

T.A.U. Group: *project for La Villette
quarter, Paris, 1976.*

T.A.U. Group: *urban scheme in
Rochefort-sur-Mer, the railroad station
square, 1977.*
Jas Bigniew: *project for the Technical
University, Warsaw, rubbish dump.*

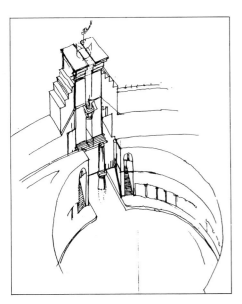

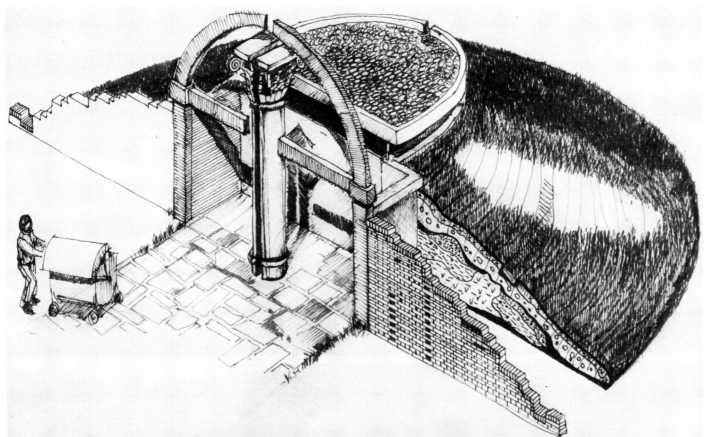

Yasufumi Kijima: *Matsuo Shrine,*
Kumanoto, 1975.
Yasufumi Kijima: *AIJ project, 1980.*

Architecture and Place

In order to seriously study the balances that regulate the life of beavers, bees or termites, no one would doubt the necessity of analyzing the way in which these animals transform the earth to create conditions for living and reproduction which would be impossible without these transformations. These transformations are often not limited to the building of the nest or den, but involve complex relationships with the environment. It is difficult for us to realize that architecture (stripping this term for a moment of its academic and theoretical connotations, and returning to its meaning in the ancient world: art, or the craft of transforming the earth in function of man's needs) is an essential element in the formation of the balance between man and the environment, and that it is hard to fully understand the meaning and value of architecture if its role as mediator between man and the world is not considered. It is true that man, unique among living creatures, possesses the greatest possibility of adapting to new balances and putting them into crisis, and renewing them for autonomous reasons; this does not authorize us, however, to believe that it is useless to study and understand the equilibria of the artificial environment. In its historic forms, this environment contains centuries of slowly stratified experiences, and therefore carries on a dialogue from afar, through the products of work, of generations following one another in the care and renewal of a sort of beneficial alliance with the places of the earth. The most eloquent and significant symbol of this alliance between man and place in which work is the catalyst, is the material that the place, in its geographic determinations, puts at the disposal of our hands as a primary factor of all its possible transformations. This is the "raw material" which makes up the natural world we see, and which will in turn "make" the other world, the artificial world we will fashion to make nature a friend, or at least an ally, from whom we should have learned to defend ourselves from the beginning.

The raw and dominant material of a place — sand, earth or stone —·is the matrix of all architecture, of every "material" culture: it has been a determining influence on perception, and has formed the sensibility of the people who succeeded one another in that place from generation to generation. Architecture, using that material, has multiplied and institutionalized its role, making it the basic ingredient of that second nature that is the earth transformed by man. World statistics tell us, surprisingly enough, that the most diffused building material today is neither reinforced concrete nor steel, but worked earth, mud. The modern world has not been able to supplant archaic building methods except in a relatively small area where technological civilization celebrates its rites, and now witnesses the fall of its redeeming illusions. What was once considered progress, the progressive cancellation of all ties with the past and hence with all preindustrial techniques, appears today as an absurd waste that risks producing a tragic process of homologation, cancelling even those differences between places and communities that were an inseparable part of their identity. Now is the time, then, to turn our renewed attention to the study of the roots tying man to the places of the earth; it is time to relearn, as if from a lost primer, the grammatical rules governing the language of places which make it recognizable and familiar. The earth worked by primitive man to build his shelter changes from place to place only in texture and color, and allows for minimal differentiation tied to processes of workmanship. Stone, on the other hand, with its solidity and the permanence of its forms, with the differentiated characteristics of its resistance, besides texture and color, imposes a "difference," carves out a furrow between the architectonic culture of neighboring regions.

I was born in the Latium region of Italy, and I remember having discovered as a boy the profound difference between the culture of tufa of the volcanic zones north of Rome, and the culture of the calcareous rock of southern Latium. Often almost as soft as earth, tufa induces behavior and produces morphologies extremely different from those of limestone. Tufa is excavated everywhere, and when the foundation of a house is dug, blocks are extracted that will be used to raise the walls. In front of the house, water can be conducted or easily collected by carving out thin tracks, canals, declivities that will eventually be smoothed out like forms in a microlandscape. Limestone, with its silvery brilliance and the hardness of its edges, does not produce unity in the complex masonry structure, but separation, fragmentation, and it is bound with mortar without fusing. Limestone landscapes have a dryness about them, a cold touch, an often vitreous glaze and lucidity that differs enormously from earthy heat, from the organic porousness of damp and spongy tufa. By observing these recurring characteristics, I learned to distinguish homogeneous areas according to a culture of

60 rock, as important as the culture of dialects. I also learned to make relationships between the building materials of certain areas and the dominant colors of the building, since stone influences architecture indirectly, too, even when it can not be used because of the high cost of excavating or working it. In this case, the colors of the plaster will echo it by reproducing the symbolic tonalities in tonal combinations of different materials. The color of a city, with its variations and dominating colors, is formed over the centuries according to the raw materials and their original appearance and the shades they take on over the years. Rome, full of earthy and violet colors and osseous tonalities, is a city marked by the presence and influence of its original materials: the tufa of the hills on which it was founded, along with travertine, pozzolana, peperino, and sperone, whose colors intentionally contrast with the blue of the sky.

I discovered lava as a construction material in Naples, when I wondered about those heavy and courageous grey plasters so common in its public buildings. I found out that the memory of lava is present quite frequently in monuments like the Palazzo Reale or the Castel dell'Ovo, where it contrasts beautifully with brick or with the ochre of tufa.

But the place where lava has absolute domination is the area around Mt. Etna, in a group of towns between the mountain and the sea. There, it is transformed from a dramatic and threatening presence into a "design," into a precious ingredient of a lean and elegant architecture using the clear contrast between light and dark and the compact rugged hardness of a material to give a solemn simplicity to the scenario of daily life.

The Teatro del Mondo

In the Teatro del Mondo realized by Aldo Rossi for the Venice Biennale, many of the characteristic themes of his architecture come together. Here, a new page is opened in a focused, coherent search capable of development and periodic renewal, through the acquisition of new types and qualities, into that "rigid world of few objects." The novelty in respect to other architecture designed by Rossi which relates the Teatro del Mondo to the small scientific theater and to his most imaginary designs is the psychological effect that the form (especially the silhouette) and materials (the warm color of wood, the blue of the sky transferred onto the terminal fillets) have on the observer. Rossi's conciseness does not contradict itself, but increasingly loses an elective tie with the austere whitish cartilage of the functionalist lexicon.

Let us first recall the genesis of this small organism. In July 1979, after the structure of the exhibition "Venice and Scenic Space" had been worked out, Rossi became interested in designing a Teatro del Mondo which would evoke the sixteenth-century tradition of theatrical floats. Even before putting together a documentation of prototypes by Rusconi and Scamozzi, Rossi had already chosen the morphological theme. It would be both a tower and a theater in the most elementary sense of the word: a contained space, not just a floating stage. It would have to be measured against the monuments of the San Marco basin. My first meeting with Aldo took place in his Milan office in early July, when the theater already has a complete form, which had matured in antithesis rather than in analogy to sixteenth-century models. It was, in fact, already a cubic container, a covering of an exactly corresponding interior space. It already has a polygonal cupola (the number of whose sides would oscillate in the early versions between six, eight, and sixteen) and two small towers for stairs at first closed, like those of Palladio and Longhena, by conical or pyramidal coverings. A change in statics was made in August, during the first meeting between the architect and the skilled workers who would build the theater. The stalls, at first placed to one side, were divided, giving the scenic space the definitive form of a corridor placed between two facing staircases. One of Rossi's strongest analogies with his earlier works is thus reduced, the reference to the staircase fitted into the cube of the monument in Cuneo. There are other significant relationships: the cabins of the Chieti project, the polygonal prism with pyramidal covering in the project for the directional center of Florence, taken from the prototype of the Baptistry, the square window divided into a cross, the sphere and crowning banner recurrent in his latest work.

The structure first imagined for the theater of the world was not to be finally realized in metal tubing, but in wood or metal carpentry, to facilitate the disassembly or reassembly of the piece, following in the Venetian tradition of the pavilions that were reassembled each year for the fair of the "Sensa." Deadlines necessitated the adoption of a redundant structure, such as the tubing. But Rossi did not sell his soul in accepting this change. It was not a constraint to him, but a stimulus to "solve" the problem according to the implacable logic of the architectural object, already defined by its exterior covering. A contradiction thus arose between the bearing structure and the roof. This problem did not exist in the original work, of which Rossi took advantage in his capacity as "engineer," in the old sense of the word, and especially as it was used in the eighteenth-century, when technical competence and the capacity to design at the building site had not yet given way to the present specialized divisions. An obvious proof of this capacity lies in the design of the interior portals built to mediate the passage between the two staircases and the stalls, where the wooden cornice becomes the archetypal sign capable of transforming the openings of the metal structure into architectural parts. Rossi followed the realization of this work with the passion and enthusiasm dictated by the exceptional nature of the theme and the place, always part of his world of images. His immediate and profitable dialogue with the carpenters, fitters, and tinsmiths derives from his joy of building. Certain details, strangely elaborate even in their simplicity, like the outriggers on the edges of the pyramidal roof that add a kind of fairy-tale feeling of fifteenth-century illuminiated manuscripts to the Teatro del Mondo, result from an immediate understanding between the people, the architect, and the tinsmith, still capable of using a common language. We spoke about a difference, or shift perceptible in the form of the Teatro del Mondo. If the theme of the material presence of wood and its minute texture can be considered the result of a construction choice, the same can not be said of the blue strip which Rossi had wanted from the start to mark the termination of the cubic volume under the cupola, and the octagonal cylinder under the pyramid revetted in

Aldo Rossi, Gianni Braghieri: *Teatro del Mondo, Venice, 1979, leaving the building site.*

Aldo Rossi, Gianni Braghieri: *Teatro del Mondo, Venice, 1979, interior viewed from below.*

64 plate. This fillet, to be sure, answers a pictorial need, since it projects the color of the sky onto the volumes. But it also tends to establish a hierarchy of superimposed parts, and therefore becomes a form analogous to the classical cornice. Rossi's completely new interests in the problem of a stratification of parts, analogous to the classical order, appears clearly also in the slightly earlier project for Cannaregio, where he used a real cornice with molding and a single angular corbel above a large brick wall marked by tiny square windows, like an ancient wall pierced by holes left from wooden scaffolding.

Perhaps it is not by chance that Rossi chose to introduce the image of the theater in the background of a drawing for Cannaregio, where a wall crowned by a cornice appears in the foreground. Both projects, in our view, signal a recourse to a freer and more open historical memory, always filtered through the rigorous inventory of typical forms. This historical memory can now be enriched beyond the limits of any modernist orthodoxy, and can combine dissonances with accords, and amplify the play of "associations." It then becomes the central moment of the project, which also becomes the project of future mnemonic operations in the mind of the observer. "These analogies of place in designing a building," Rossi wrote in presenting the Teatro, "are extremely important to me. If read correctly, they are themselves the project." There is a margin of stimulating ambiguity in this sentence: who in fact is to "read correctly" the analogies, the architect in his memory, or the observer who decodes the object before his eyes? Or is "reading correctly" an operation that unites author and observer in an imaginary dialogue that occurs through the signs of the work and allows the reconstruction of the project, the formation of the image in the mind? Each of these interpretations focuses on a process of communication, whose intensity is dictated by the degree of levigation of the form, reduced to a minimum common denominator, a common emotional resonance rooted in the unconscious and in the collective memory.

In addition to all the "associations" so lucidly proposed by Rossi for his theater in the essay he wrote for the catalogue of the exhibition "Venice and Scenic Space," I believe we should also consider a probably non-intentional but no less meaningful analogy: that of the painted architecture of Carpaccio, and more generally, of the category of painted architecture from Giotto to de Chirico. The analogy has a superficial level in the wooden revetment with its vertical texture, recalling the image of the bridge on the Grand Canal in the work by Carpaccio dedicated to the "Patriarch of Grado who frees a demoniac," the same crude definition of volumetric contours set against the background of "Venetian" architecture, with its pinnacles, fringed contours, and surfaces that breathe through the cyclical concentration of the openings. Tafuri has written that the homage to the sense of limit, to the Albertian concept of the *finitio* contained in the little theater is "specifically anti-Venetian." Instead, it seems to me proof of how Rossi's historical readings have little to do with clichés, and with the generic definition, and how they point to the contradictions that give life and depth to the language of places. An observation of the protagonists of the San Marco basin helps us to understand their specific environmental character, not as a monotonous celebration of the "fluidity of space," but as a harmonic antithesis of blocked volumes, of closed forms lacking adjectives, and complex sculptural germinations developed vertically, reverberations in stone of a process of "evaporation" constantly suggested by water in its cycle of transformations. Palladio certainly did not invent this dialectic, expressed in its highest form in the Palazzo Ducale, and before that in San Marco in its original form. The polarity between pure forms and sculptural fraying is also present in a Baroque building like the church of the Salute, where the doubling of the dome gives two antithetical versions of the theme, and also gives life to an architectural dialogue between simplicity and complexity.

Rossi chose blocked volumes, but extended them vertically (that he was aware of the need to listen to both the calling of the created object and the calling of the place is evident in his insistence on not going below the height of twenty meters). He has demonstrated an understanding of the profound structures of Venice with that infallible factor of truth, the creative intelligence. But the most intriguing analogy with painted architecture, discussed by others before, has to do with the "metaphysical" quality assumed by architecture in the tradition which goes from Pompeian painting to de Chirico. Until now, this analogy had found a conscious echo in built architecture only rarely, in a series of examples from Taramello to Genga, from Borromini to Boullée, Garnier, Muzio, Gigiotti Zanini, to name just a few.

Undoubtedly, some of de Chirico's thoughts from the time of *Valori Plastici* can shed some light on Rossi's operation and its diversity and specificity in a metaphysical sense that cultivates the banal collective sense of the city and of form. It is therefore worthwhile to reread these reflections, using them as keys that can turn in opposite directions. "I remember the strange and deep impression I had as a child upon seeing an illustration in an old book called *Earth Before the Flood*," wrote de Chirico. "It was a picture of a landscape of the Tertiary Era. Man did not yet exist. I have often meditated upon this strange phenomenon of the *human absence* in the metaphysical sense. Every profound work of art contains two solitudes: one that could be called *plastic solitude*, that contemplative beatitude that gives us the genial construction and combination of forms (materials and dead-alive or alive-dead elements; the second life of still-lifes, understood not as a subject in painting, but as a spectral aspect that might even be that of a supposed living figure); the second solitude is that of signs. There are paintings by Boecklin, Claude Lorrain, and Poussin inhabited by human figures which are closely connected to the landscape of the Tertiary Era. Human absence in man. Certain portraits by Ingres attain this."

"Human absence in man:" something of this alienating effect belongs to Rossi's architecture, giving the human figure the relief of a silhouette, the immobility of a model. But Rossi's thesis is that this solitude of signs is also the condition necessary for making the flow of "warm life" run in this river bed without viscosity, in a situation of absolute detachment and clarity. De Chirico makes his most enlightening comments with respect to Rossi's architecture when speaking about Giotto. Five years ago, I spoke with de Chirico about Rossi, about whom he knew nothing, or at least pretended not to. I managed to shake up his ironic indifference, and caused him to reflect on architecture by reminding him of the essay he published in the June 1920 issue of *Valori Plastici* concerning the "architectural sense in ancient painting." "All openings (doors, arcades, windows)," de Chirico wrote, "that accompany the figures, allow for a premonition of the cosmic mystery. The square of the sky bounded by the lines of a window is a second drama caught up in the human drama. More than one disturbing question comes up when the eye meets those blue or greenish surfaces, closed off by the lines of geometricized stone — what is over there?... Is there a deserted sea beneath that sky, or a crowded city? Or does that sky extend over free and restless nature, over wooded mountains, dark valleys, plains carved out by rivers?... And the buildings rise, full of mystery and premonitions, the corners conceal secrets, and the work of art is no longer the dry episode, the scene limited to the acts of people depicted, but the whole cosmic and vital drama that entangles man in its spirals, where past and future are confused, where the enigmas of existence... uncover the knotted and frightening aspect that man imagines for himself outside the world of art..."

The Teatro del Mondo in Venice is perhaps the only theater with a window opening onto the center of the stage. Divided into four squares, this window is both the sign and symbol of an architecture attempting to "discover the eye in everything," to help us understand, mercilessly but with trust, the meaning of the human condition.

Aldo Rossi: *entrance gate to the exhibition "The Presence of the Past," Venice, 1980.*

Aldo Rossi, Gianni Braghieri, A. Cantafora: *competition for student housing, Chieti, 1976.*

Aldo Rossi, Gianni Braghieri: *house, Borgo Ticino, 1973.*

The Crisis of the City

The metropolis leads toward the megalopolis, which leads sooner or later to the necropolis. The prophetic journey which Mumford talked about thirty years ago has not yet taken place, but continues to terrorize us. Every so often, the mechanism of the big cities seems to jam irreparably, and the ghost of urban agony comes back to haunt our dreams. Then, a balance, albeit precarious, is recomposed, as in a spell. Some scheme is devised, and what seemed very near begins to move away again.

The last of the great ghosts, the administrative and political ungovernability of large urban systems, is also being redimensioned. Some years ago, New York reported its economic bankruptcy. Cairo, Naples, and Rome have administrative balances that are hardly reassuring; but in the end, a corrective is found and the rendering of accounts deferred. In reality, it seems that a colossal regulator of watts guarantees the survival of this "splendidly" ill institution called the large city.

Its fanatics insist that this is opportune and providential, because the preservation and development of human civilization are inseparably tied to the city. Should the city disintegrate, the narrow-minded and conservative spirit of the small town would suddenly arrest the prodigious critical vigor that generated the modern world. The big city is where exchanges, meetings, opportunities for intellectual growth and scientific research take place, where social tensions and intellectual ferment are created and constantly changed. While it does not necessarily grant happiness and serenity, the city guarantees that intense, rich and complex life "that is worth living."

What are the true and false elements of this rhetoric of urban greatness according to which quantity would be miraculously transformed into quality, and difficulties would become stimuli for the life of the intellect? We could begin to give some answers to this question, since the mythological phase of the modern world is ending. Every day, we witness the collapse and changes of the great central systems with which we deluded ourselves that everything could be explained.

The large city is the child of the great political institutions, beginning with the advent of capitalism, of the great productive organizations that benefit from physical contiguity, because in this manner the mechanism of the market and of competition is mirrored most directly in the urban fabric. The large city is essentially a city-factory, a city-workshop, where a gigantic invisible assembly line compels everyone to repeat daily both the ceremony of work, and an infinite series of useless acts. Slow and discontinuous vehicular traffic, periodically grinding to a maddening halt, and then gradually decongested into the still of the night, is the eloquent symbol of the sacrifices that must be made so that we can enjoy the privileges of its function as a great devourer of human time and a great machine of waste. What will become of this institution which has derived force from its illness, and which continues, like a siren, to attract its distant admirers with false promises? There is no doubt that the myth of infinite development (hypothesized in the sixties when the generalization of urban systems like that of Tokyo were considered) is in difficulty. The myth-antidote of zero growth was also invented. The salvation of the large city lies in its controlled growth and its ties with the surrounding territory. But it also lies, paradoxically, in a complete alternative that would make its advantages accessible to a wider range of people and progressively weaken its force of attraction.

It is clear, now more than ever, that even for the large cities, egotism is a double-edged weapon. The concentration of public facilities, cultural institutions, places for recreation and scientific elaboration has given the metropolis the glory of two centuries, but in the long run it could have bad surprises in store. The cure for the sick metropolis lies perhaps in the potential of the smaller city, in the rediscovery of its competitive role in the field of culture and production. This new possibility has come up recently, with the generalization of the means of mass communication that increase the demand for services and collective institutions, precisely because the ruling culture of the big city makes its standards accessible at the level of the image and desire.

Postindustrial society (if we can advance a hypothesis) will no longer need great convulsive concentrations and *villes tentaculaires*, just as modern industry no longer needs cathedrals of work. Small cities will once again play a role not only in the consumption and passive reception of the culture of the metropolis, but also in autonomous creation and valid interlocution. The small centers, where a great part of the world's population still lives, will be able to find a competitive role in their refound autonomous identity, and in the process of federation which will permit them to develop sufficient force to give the new territory community structures similar to urban ones. A

Paolo Portoghesi, Giampaolo Ercolani,
Giovanna Massobrio: *commercial agrarian
center for Vallo di Diano, 1979.*

70   process of this type, the union of nineteen neighboring towns into a single town of "urban force," is taking place in Italy south of Salerno in the Vallo di Diano, through the initiative of the enlightened administrator Gerardo Ritorto. I have made a technical contribution to the development of this interesting hypothesis of a discontinuous city.

It is believed that postindustrial society will be completely free from totalitarian temptations. The postmodern culture which arises from the new human condition produced by this society ought to defeat on another level even urban totalitarianism, separating the positive values of the big city from its negative connotations that have shaped a relationship of exploitation and alienating hegemony between the culture of the city and that of the region. For Italy, it would be the rediscovery of a very old calling. The old Italy of the courts could become the polycentric Italy of the "small city."

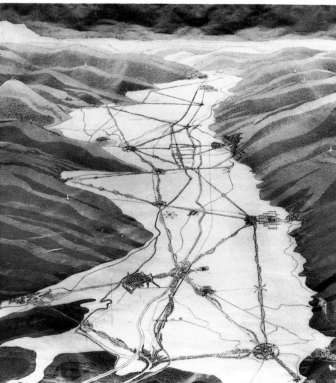

Paolo Portoghesi, Giampaolo Ercolani,
Giovanna Massobrio: *headquarters of the
Local Health Department, Vallo di Diano,
1980–1981.*

The Postindustrial City Between Zeal and Indolence

It has been almost a century and a half since Augustus Welby Northmore Pugin, illustrating his "contrasts," drew two images of the same city next to one another, represented in the Middle Ages and the present. The comparison then, as today, contained an explosive critical charge. It contrasted a confused urban landscape of little structural quality, stripped of its symbolic capacities, with another urban landscape corresponding to a "dark" age in history, though happily adhering to the ideals and values of the society which produced it, and endowed with an exemplary order and clarity. The medieval city is like a big house where everything has its place: the buildings destined to collective functions dominate the arrangement of private dwellings, and each building has its own identity, while the destination of its interior spaces is recognizable from a distance. In Pugin's image of 1834, the modern city has already undergone what Pasolini called the process of homologation: public and private buildings distinguish themselves neither for their size nor height, and smokestacks and steeples become confused, while the dwellings of the lower classes have taken the form of lazarettos.

Another engraving illustrates the differences between the dwellings of the poor, in a series of vignettes that extend the comparison to other aspects of life: the landlord, the master, the diet, the funeral, and forced discipline.

Pugin reacted to the degradation of the city as a social institution after the advent of industrial production. He tried to change the course of this barbarization by working on a completely superstructural aspect: architectural style. His rebellion began that movement of collective consciousness which took the name Modern Movement, that has struggled for decades in a crisis that will be resolved only by a radical change of course.

The situation today, if we were to reproduce the contrast between the ancient city and the new city, or the contrast between historic center and periphery, has changed only for the worse. The city we live in is much worse than the society in which we live.

It is true that respect for man's rights has made some progress. Social inequalities are fewer, the access to knowledge has spread incredibly, and technology has made available unforeseen forces and possibilities. Our cities have, however, lost the capacity to express the values of society, collective wishes, and the role of institutions. If we disregard some eloquent but pathological examples of urban rhetoric such as New York, modern cities express the silence of institutions, the confusion of forces, and the eclipse of the quality and the representativity of architecture. For the last fifty years, there has been an increase in the process of impoverishment, with a kind of masochistic connivance on the part of architectural culture.

And yet, although the symptoms of an awakening are still concealed and inhibited by all kinds of conservatism, it is possible today to think about an inversion of tendency with respect to the destiny of the cities. This diagnosis derives not from prophecies or unfounded dreams, but from a serious study of the processes of transformation occurring in the technical, economic, and cultural fields. Such changes are marking the gradual passage from an industrial society, for which progress is equal to infinite and accelerated development, to a postindustrial society. On the ashes of the mythological equation development =progress, the idea of the importance of "limit" and controls is gaining ground, according to which the progressiveness of economic development can be the object of a careful evaluation, and its reverberations studied for the most part with methods of probability.

It would certainly be naïve and wrong to believe that instruments of control and forecast can substitute the logic of profit with that of universal well-being. But it is also true that the logic of profit is not the only one in force within the limits of the system. The distribution of power, no longer definable according to Marx's elementary scheme, reveals, in that logic of spaces, the existence of wide breaks where even intellectual work can be inserted as an alternative instrument of concrete struggle.

Foucault has taught us that a total revolutionary strategy does not exist, and that limited determined partial struggles have more effect upon changing the world. "We know," André Gorz has written, "that society will never be 'good' by virtue of its organization, but only by reason of the spaces of autonomy, self-organization, and voluntary cooperation that it offers to individuals."

The advanced industrial city, which had the Modern Movement as its ideological patrimony, experienced the irresolvable contradiction between the control of ideology and plan, and the will of the economic power of the bureaucratic state. The postindustrial city, on the other hand, is moving toward partial transformations, corrections of tendency based on a culture of complexity, stripped of totalitarian ambitions, and above all finally deprived of the mirror of ideology understood as a false conscience that forces us to justify every choice in the area of an illusory general project.

With regard to a policy of the restoration, renewal, and replanning of the city, we will search for what Touraine has called "spaces without norms," that react to the extraordinary capacity typical of the bureaucratic apparatus to make norms for their own ends, spaces in which people will be able to recognize their aspiration to the development of a free personality.

The postindustrial city will be generated by a world where economics alone will no longer furnish models, since the level of culture has revealed the neuralgic level of transformation, contradictions, and struggles, and it seems that it will continue to do so.

The nature of the domination exercised by the apparatus on the whole of society is more subtle than economic "exploitation." These apparatus produce models of behavior more than goods, culture rather than machines. Fighting against degenerations of technocratic power means fighting within, and for, culture.

The postindustrial city will be the product of a clash, but also of a collaboration possible between the great apparatus and democratic forces. It will be the product of a pact whose object is culture, and which should not escape the critical control and creative contribution of the intellectuals. If we can use Pugin's comparison in the reverse, it is possible that in the new city, rising not from the ashes of the old, but on its structures which have been reinterpreted, transformed, and enriched, there will once again be emerging symbols of the collective life, strong structures whose identity facilitates orientation and fruition; containing spaces, like ancient cities, able to inspire the intensity of social relationships, "spaces without norms" in which the historical process can be read, and experimental spaces in which the tension toward the unknown is expressed.

We live in the information age, and we will learn to read the city as a system of signs, a whole of possible itineraries, from the daily itinerary to the contemplative one of the tourist. These routes must intertwine not by chance, and act on the city with the cautiousness of the farmer who carries out his grafting, making diversity possible in continuity.

The culture of the protest movements of the sixties posed

A.W.N. Pugin: *engravings of the medieval and nineteenth-century cities, from* Contrasts, *London, 1841.*
Gallaratese quarter, Milan.

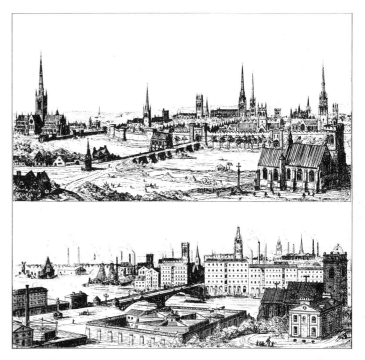

Paolo Portoghesi, Giampaolo Ercolani,
Giovanna Massobrio: *thermal center in
Canino, second project, 1981.*

in clear terms the problem *of the right to the city*, of the reconquest on the part of everyone of the environment, of collective services, of the places of production and cultural consumption, which make up the identity of the great urban tradition, even if no concrete solutions were offered. The theme was taken up again in different forms. On the incentive of the struggles for the territory, a new demand grew for a culture of unforeseeable dimensions. As far as the right to the city is concerned, however, little progress has been made, and the spectacular reappropriation of certain urban spaces, seen in historical perspective, resembles a cloud of smoke.

The city continues to exist and to grow as center and periphery: the place of the daily spectacle and the daily hardship, of stacked up dormitories, of the secluded spaces of apartments. For the consumption of this immobilism caused by urban policy, culture has created the myth of the "historic center" that Italy has cultivated to the point of producing it for export. Preservation without choices and priorities has been mythicized: preserve everything in words, but actually administer corruption, degradation, and misuse. The connection between the old urban fabric and the lower classes has been idealized, making even more difficult the rehabilitation of old structures, and undervaluing the importance of the intertwining of productive activities that give urban centers their unmistakable character. The concept of the "historic center" has broken the continuity between city and territory, ignoring the historic aspects of the landscape and the complexity of relationships by which it is expressed. At the same time, the division of roles between the old and new parts of the city has been guaranteed.

In the old city, values are lodged, the collective identity is celebrated, and much space is given to esthetic problems. In the new city, primary needs are administered, translated into cubic feet of cement, into houses joined to others with no facilities, except those prescribed by the myopia of town planning standards, without the least attention to spontaneously formed communities, and the regional origin of immigrants.

In light of these considerations, the balance of the spectacular wave that hit the historic centers appears not only as a palliative to the problem of the right to the city. It is also a dangerous retardant to the relaunching of collective values in urban life. This is true since this balance conceals, under the glare of spotlights, the absence and

eclipse of those institutions that are the only acceptable mediation in a democratic society between cultural production and consumption. It may well be that for that particular culture of the elite, which finds so much room in the Italian Communist Party, this recourse to advertising logic applied to the cultural product is acceptable because it is useful, and profitable from an electoral point of view. An attitude of this kind would be in tune with the revisitation of negative thought and with the disappointed conscience that substitutes the obliging proof of the degradation of bourgeois culture, of its reduction to the mass consumption of the "already produced" for the removed revolution, against the reformist temptation that homologates communism with the social democratic tradition. For some years now, certain communist intellectuals have accustomed us to a total pessimism, indicating as an inevitable "scheme of capital" the devaluation and destruction of the cognitive value of intellectual work. They have left room only for the critique of ideology, which has become the critique of "unmasking," a moralistic litany on the recurrent sins of the intellectuals, condemning to silence any possible propositional or creative intervention. The moralistic austerity of this weighted down criticism, based on Marxism as a principle of authority, is actually the other side of the spectacular and acritical use of cultural consumption. Both choices derive from a profound distrust in institutional construction and in reformism, and postulate the separation of culture into two parts, waiting for a mythical and distant reconciliation. If all this is acceptable from the point of view of negative thought, it certainly is not from the point of view of a new libertarian reformism, and it is necessary more than ever that someone who is part of this trend offer precise and courageous indications on the theme of the city.

Another exciting prospect in the postindustrial picture is that of rebalancing the conflict between city and countryside, between large and small settlements. It is not by chance that in a geographic area in southern Italy with a strong socialist presence, the federative hypothesis of the Città Vallo di Diano arose, proposing the administrative fusion of nineteen small towns into a single municipality, with the objective of creating an urban force of the ideal size of one hundred thousand inhabitants.

The right to the city is not a luxury to be distributed through cultural cooperatives like hand-outs in a soup

Paolo Portoghesi: *Enel housing, Tarquinia,*
1982.

kitchen: the right to the city will be satisfied only by reforming the present city, by viewing it once again as an organic unity, in which collective values are not preserved in the safes of the historic center, but circulate around the entire urban network. This means totally replanning the periphery, and building no more dormitories according to the obsolete principles of the separation of functions so dear to Le Corbusier's Athens Charter, and giving sense back to already existing dormitories according to the obsolete principles of the separation of functions so dear to Le Corbusier's Athens collective life. In these forums, new building types must find a place that can interpret in institutional terms the new demand for culture and happiness, and the new needs of communication and recreation. Bourgeois society in ascent was able to give a stable form to its own needs through the creation of buildings like the theater, the public gallery, the museum and the library. Our present society, profoundly transformed by the fall of the barriers of privilege and by the technological and psychological information revolution, is still waiting for someone to creatively interpret these differences that mark the passage between an industrial civilization, homologated on the model of mechanical production, and a postindustrial civilization, which tries to put man back at the center of his vision of the world.

Italian civilization is primarily polycentric. Our land is one of cities, jealous of their own identity and size. No political unification has been able to level these differences. Today, basic conditions exist permitting every city to regain its identity and produce culture once again, which will be an international culture if it understands how to evaluate its own identity and its own ties with the place.

This relaunching of Italian polycentrism must become an organic part of a conscious political program, and must express itself in terms of the courage to undertake new institutional planning.

For years, a scattered and labored debate has forced us to discuss Biennales, Triennales and Quadriennales, as if they were ghosts to bring back to life. But what has been done to give our society the means of reflecting upon itself and creating something closer to its needs?

The cultural calling of every Italian city should be studied and understood through structures that render cultural activity permanent and productive.

From a postindustrial viewpoint, the increasing role of the service sectors of cities could become an hypothesis of the rebirth and liberation of vital forces: those forces which every political program must take into account if it is not be simply a dry and not very forward-looking organization of consensus.

Grand Avenue in Los Angeles

78 Today, the new architecture rising from the ashes of modernism is going through the same thing that happened to modern architecture in its infancy in the second decade of this century. The conservatives are trying in every way to block its growth, taking advantage of large competitions to loudly reject projects that could "define an age" and verify the hypotheses of renewal. This happened at the time of the competition for the headquarters of the League of Nations in Geneva, when a beautiful project by Le Corbusier lost to a bad Italian project. Something similar is now happening in Los Angeles in the Bunker Hill competition. A conventional solution by the Erikson group, using the obsolete principles of the International Style, was preferred to the project by a prestigious team led by Robert Maguire, with the collaboration of Charles Moore, Cesar Pelli, Barton Myers, Lawrence Halprin, Frank Gehry and Norman Pfeiffer.

The Maguire project was based on very clear sociological and urbanistic premises in line with the most advanced studies in the field of environmental quality. Instead of proposing the usual homogeneous complex of nicely arranged glass cubes, it tried to create a "piece of a city" with all the typical characteristics of the traditional urban fabric: complexity, variety, and interweaving of different functions, the richness of spaces suitable for walking, stopping and being together both inside and outside the buildings and the multiplicity of styles and forms. Recognizing the fact that a city designed by one architect alone is like an orchestra made up of only one instrument, and that harmonies and contradictions are necessary to obtain the effect of a real city, Maguire put together a heterogeneous group of people who know their craft well, and who have contributed in various ways to the renewal of architectural language. The result is convincing precisely for its apparent incoherence. Perhaps for the first time, an American city would have been given an "urban theater" comparable to one of the spatial sequences of Baroque cities.

Moore and Pelli in particular demonstrated their exceptional design capacities. Moore organized contemplative parentheses in different points of the street, playing with

Hill Street Elevation

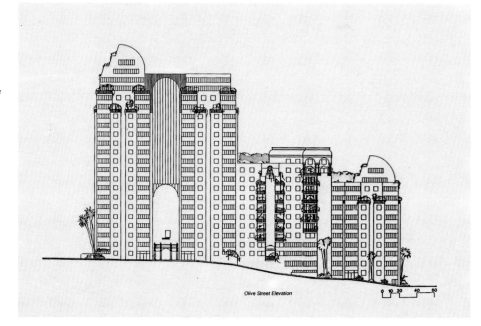

Olive Street Elevation

Maguire Group: *four views of the project for Grand Avenue, Los Angeles, 1980.*

water, perspective and light. Pelli designed   79
open towers perfectly clear like rock
crystals, studied to enrich the landscape
with surprising spatial situations.
The refusal of the Grand Avenue, solemnly
expressed by the bureaucrats of Los
Angeles against the opinion of many
journalists, is a coup that compromises the
future of the city, condemning it to the
repetition of errors made in the past. The
same thing happened in Italy with regard to
the city of Schio, where the worst projects
were premiated, and all those adhering to
the new tendencies were ignored. But a
wave is not forced back with a stroke of the
oars, and the revolt against what was called
"modern" is spreading beyond the
boundaries of this discipline.

Queensgate in Cincinnati

Modern cities, or rather, the modern
quarters around cities, need to be
redesigned. This is the inevitable conclusion
of any attempt at a balance that is not
obfuscated by the caste spirit of architects
and city planners. These quarters must be
redesigned. With rare exceptions, cities
have grown through the construction of
great collective dormitories with the a
posteriori addition of insufficient services
programatically detached from the
residences. This disintegrated whole of the
traditional ingredients of the city has
produced something unpleasant, as in a
mayonnaise in which a lack of
amalgamation prevents the formation of the
characteristic taste of the sauce. Modern
neighborhoods lack precisely this taste of
the city. For this reason, that horrible term
"periphery" is given to them, which
immediately evokes boredom, squalor,
melancholy, and irremediable human
solitude.

The latest generation of architects has
concentrated on the theme of the redesign
of the periphery of the city, in order to
transform it into a part of the city. To
indicate this objective, architects have
recently adopted the category of
urbanization, in polemic with the totalizing
tradition of city planning. Urbanization is
both an old and a new need, and one that
is growing. The urban and regional
struggles that claim the need for centers of
regrouping capable of reversing the process
of the disintegration of the periphery are
proof of this.

In Cincinnati, Ohio, a participatory process
for a facilities center deserves mention both
as a symptom of a pressing request from the
people for urban quality, and for its result,
which can be placed within the postmodern
problematic. It all began in 1971 with a
popular protest against the leveling of a
part of the city to make way for one of the
usual gigantic urban highways. In exchange,
homes for the displaced and the
construction of a new civic center were
won, right at the boundary of two
neighborhoods, one black and one white.
A series of projects was used as a basis for
a discussion of the needs and wishes of the
inhabitants during public assemblies. A
complex model emerged, in which different
activities could be held, a kind of medieval
piazza that could be transformed into a

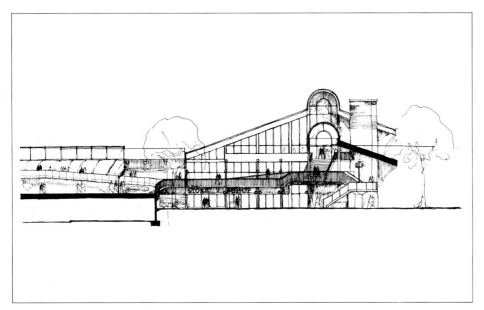

theater, to bring together commerce,   81
culture, entertainment, contemplation, and
lounging, a piece of the city on a human
scale where the automobile is kept to one
side, and where the inhabitants are the
protagonists. Naturally, the collective
memory was consulted, and discussions with
the future users of the site set simple ideas
into circulation once again, which the
architects might have disregarded. Since
this was a "center," a circular form was
chosen, around which steps rise as in an
ancient theater. A covered passageway, a
"portico," a covered domed space and a
"kiosk" are the main elements, dusted off
from the repertoire of the popular
imagination. At Queensgate II, the modern
city emerges from its falsely austere
muteness and begins speaking once again,
perhaps stuttering. But this time, the Dada
is for everyone. It is not just the cry of rage
of a minority of intellectuals who want to
teach others how to live, and who celebrate
only their own solitude and separateness.

Philip Johnson

Philip Johnson: *project for the skyscraper for P.P.G. Industries, Pittsburgh, 1980.*

Philip Johnson: *United Bank Center, Denver (Col.), 1980.*

Philip Johnson: *Community Church, Garden Grove (Ca.), 1981.*

82 Philip Johnson seems determined to disappoint anyone who tries to place him within binding tendencies or categories. To anyone who considers him a "neoclassic," his latest church built in Garden Grove, California, must seem like heresy; while some believers in the old Modernism will delight in thinking that the building, all glass and steel, is a reconversion to the other orthodoxy of Modernism. The truth is that Johnson is really going through a great period of creativity which derives its meaning and worth from the very indifference and interchangeability of languages, from the discovery of the aridity and datedness of projects which look only toward coherence and toward the construction of a personal style lacking contradictions and openings. The recourse to traditional compositional forms and methods has, paradoxically, given the architect a new security and capacity for control in using the linguistic repertoire tied to modern technology.

The church in Garden Grove is polygonal in form with a mirrored exterior, which the image of the sky penetrates dramatically, as Gordon Schenck's marvelous photograph shows. This strategem recalls a painting by Magritte and introduces a very evident symbolic connotation into the image. The skin covering the whole volume lets the rays of the sun pass through to the interior, where they are filtered and broken up. Under this skin, the very light reticular structure forms a sort of vibrating lace made soft and evanescent and then geometrically crude by the variations of the luminous flux.

Technology and morphology are used, but completely outside the tradition of the Modern Movement, because it is the image that precedes and determines the process of technical realization.

The Gothic rhythm of the great serial openings is transformed into a uniform fabric by the transparency, while the infinite quantity of small elements that form the bearing structure suggests the memory of a natural structure like a gigantic rock cave.

On the exterior, the structural motif is expressed in only one point, the highest, where it becomes ornament and sign, like a great Gothic portal. Johnson lets the "presence of the past" filter through, but

Philip Johnson: *the architect's studio, New Canaan, 1978.*

84   this does not stop him from making use of the fragments most charged with valences left free of the modern language of architecture, from Mies to Wright, to German Expressionism.

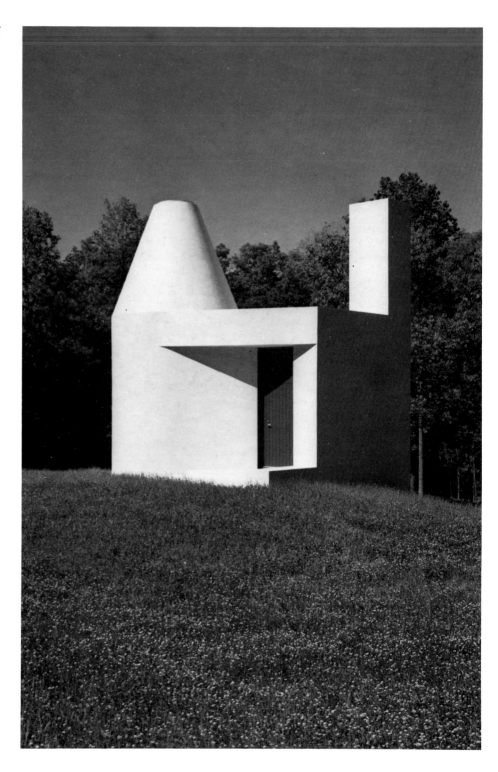

Philip Johnson: *the architect's studio, New Canaan, 1978.*

Philip Johnson: *skyscraper in San Francisco, 1980.*

Philip Johnson: *project for a skyscraper at 33 Maiden Lane, New York, elevation, 1981.*

Cesar Pelli

The career of Cesar Pelli, born in
Tucumán, Argentina in 1926, is an example
of how in the United States there still exists
a concrete connection and a possibility for
osmosis between profession and culture,
and between practical experience and
teaching. His slow but steady rise made use
of a double track: the productive
experience of the large office dealing with
industrial production, and a coherent
inquiry capable of imposing its own cultural
identity. After beginning with Eero
Saarinen in the fifties, Pelli passed to a
firm of lesser qualitative importance. In
1968, however, he began a collaboration of
much reciprocal usefulness with Gruen
Associates. This association put him into
the limelight, and led to his appointment in
1976 as head of the architecture school of
one of the most prestigious American
universities, Yale University in New Haven.
It was only the next year, when he turned
fifty, that he decided to open his own
office. Architecture is not music, and there
are no cases of extremely precocious
architects. A six-year old child can play the
piano well and can even compose good
music, but it is difficult to find clients who
would put their faith in the hands of a child
prodigy. Even Louis Kahn, not to mention
Michelangelo and Bernini, began to create
significant architecture when he was around
fifty, and this did not prevent him from
leaving his mark on the profession. Cesar
Pelli, on the other hand, even when he
worked for a large organization, had
already created considerable works, and his
complete autonomy has only intensified and
made more recognizable the quality of his
output. He thus became a protagonist of
that area between avant-garde and
industrial culture entrusted with the
incidence and fortune of intellectual
fashions. In the past several years, Pelli's
experience has focused on the
characterization and individualization of
buildings realized with the most advanced
technologies. In particular, he has
reinterpreted the theme of the skyscraper
with a new sensibility, far from the
structuralist purism of Mies, and tending
toward the recovery of certain features that
made their mark on the flowering of
skyscrapers in New York in the twenties. If
Mies sheared off the glass towers, making
them boxes with no beginning or end,

Cesar Pelli: *World Trade Center area, Battery Park, New York, 1981.*

Cesar Pelli: *Pacific Design Center, Los Angeles, 1975.*

Cesar Pelli: *project for Hermann Towers, 1981.*

Cesar Pelli: *Museum of Modern Art Tower, New York, 1980—1981.*

without what is called "perspective closure," and had eliminated all decorative whims from the glass skin destined to enclose volumes, Pelli has returned, like Johnson, to a study of the problem of the top of the building and the surfaces that enclose the box. With his Pacific Design Center in Los Angeles of 1975, he demonstrated the possibility of modelling the transparent volume until it becomes a symbolic object, in which the modelled object helps to repropose a relationship between the building and its surrounding atmosphere, between the building volume and the skyline, so important in a vertical city. The Museum of Modern Art tower reproduces, if somewhat timidly, the stepped profile of the skyscrapers of the Jazz Age. But in a project for Pittsburgh and in a more recent one for the tip of downtown Manhattan, near Yamasaki's twin towers, polyhedral and pyramidal towers once again have a dialogue with the "talking city" which had been forced into "glassy" silence by the false austerity of the fifties.

Peter Eisenman

88 Peter Eisenman, the most radical and theoretical of the New York Five who became internationally known at the beginning of the seventies, seems determined to make the beginning of a new decade coincide with a decisive turning point in his work. At the Institute for Architecture and Urban Studies, which he founded and directs (and which in New York has been mythicized as the most exclusive and up-to-date center for the cultural training of architects), his slowed down teaching activity has upset his students, colleagues and supporters. There are those who suspect that the very recent setting up of a professional office (with Christopher J. Glaister, city planning and transportation expert, and Jaqueline T. Robertson, dean of the School of Architecture of the University of Virginia) is a symptom of a change in interests. It also signals a progressive abandonment of Eisenman's prestigious role as leader of the cultural avant-garde that he chose for himself in founding the Institute, and in connecting it with the publication of *Oppositions*, the first American architectural magazine dealing with the work of a minority. In fact, in associating himself with Robertson, a recognized professional who has counted the Shah among his clients, Eisenman, in his own words, intends to "focus on and mediate between some of the greatest and most diffused conflicts typical of design and development: between public interests and private development, between esthetic rigor and social destination, between professional idealism and enlightened pragmatism, between cultural wealth and the growing constraints of the economy and environment, between new buildings and meaningful environmental situations, between technical ability and cultural aspirations, between thinking and doing." Faced with a vaster and less select clientele than that for which he built his very elegant "conceptual" houses, numbered like the works of a musician, Eisenman will no doubt be forced to give up the experimental character of the scientific laboratory of his work up to this time. But if we can judge from the first projects to come out of the new office, Eisenman will not give up his leaning toward ideology.

In criticizing the work of Michael Graves,

Eisenman wrote in *Oppositions* in 1978 that the work of the former, after his turn to Postmodernism, tried to reaffirm the "ancient values" of architectural tradition while discussing them once again, but abandoning the ideological contents of modernism.

According to Eisenman, Graves thus crosses the boundaries of orthodoxy, and in creating architecture that "speaks of its own accessibility," he abandons the "silence" of the modern work that consists in speaking only of the sacred reign of the internal structure of language.

His latest works seem to contribute to the cult of this silent reign: the project for the Berlin Friedrichstadt, recently premiated by the IBA (Berlin Internationale Bauhausstellung), the project for the

Pioneer Courthouse Square in Portland, and the skyscraper for New York, still in the design phase.

The conceptual program in Berlin dominates the plastic image in an attempt to create, not with architecture but with allusions to content, a "symbolic space of intense cultural significance." In the Portland project, the dialogue with history seems more transparent, through the evocative use of the volume of the traditional American house. In the skyscraper, the emphasis on silence returns. Its volume, built above a small building that will be preserved, is placed in the center of the area, and becomes invisible from the street, a "nonexistent knight" of architecture that recalls Calvino or Bresson.

Michael Graves

With the year 2000 drawing near, architecture is going through an extremely significant change, destined to alter profoundly the future environment of our cities. This turning point can be compared to that of a return to figurative painting after the abandonment of the tradition of abstraction. In order to really understand what the concept of figuration means in architecture, we must go back to its history. This figuration concerns not the direct imitation of nature, but rather the reproduction of a series of conventional archetypes like the hut, the wall, the column, the door, the pediment and so on. When an architect designed a façade or a door in the past, he reproduced some of these archetypes, interpreting them quite freely, inspired by a principle of order derived in large part from the form of the human body. Modern architecture tried to substitute this process with one of abstraction, based on the all-comprehensive concept of function, denying the necessity of archetypes and their imitation.

The latest generation of architects is retracing the steps of their fathers and grandfathers, and is rediscovering the process whereby novelty is not the consequence of useless, perpetual reinvention, but the result of reintegrating ancient norms which have always been in agreement with our thought processes, with the forms of the human body, and with the collective memory.

These considerations come to mind immediately when we observe one of the latest works by Michael Graves, the only architect of the famous group of the New York Five who some time ago abandoned the refined revisitations of the white architecture of the twenties, in order to participate in the great selective effort to restore a sense of history to architecture. With the Sunar Furniture Showroom in Houston, Texas, Graves has written another page in his diary of "archeologist of the future." He had to create spaces suitable for displaying furniture, giving the feeling of being inside a house, and he took advantage of this to investigate the possibilities of a new "architectural order," of a system of parts and proportions regulated by a principle of superimposition. Graves needs no decorations or mechanical quotations to make us understand that his

cylindrical elements are "columns," imitations of an archetype that has always been in our memory, and that modern architecture could not erase. The columns and the simplified cornices that connect them above serve to define the space through their proportions, and to give it a definite rhythm. Very original colors animate the structure with optical effects and reveal the division into parts. Graves was attacked for his neofigurative leanings in *Oppositions* by Peter Eisenman, his old playmate in avant-garde games, who made a play on Graves' last name by entitling his essay "The Graves of Modernism." The vitality of Graves' latest works proves, however, that new and more beautiful flowers are constantly growing over the "graves of Modernism."

If we consider that the principal interest of the language of architecture is the "metaphorical representation of man and the landscape, we could perhaps use this simple basic language to express not only simple ideas, but complex and poetic ideas as well:" this is how Michael Graves describes his work of the last few years. He speaks in the humble and ingratiating tone of someone who is advancing a hypothesis and not pretending to teach the truth. This is the exact opposite of the prophetic tone dear to the avant-garde. But his proposal is bold, and upsets the very foundations of modern language, based on the abandonment of all figuration and symbolic references. Graves intends to take up the interrupted theme of imitation, the imitation of nature and of man as a product of nature itself. Architecture involves the relationship between man and nature, and needs metaphorical references to transmit ideas. If the poet uses metaphor to define an image through analogy, charging it at the same time with ambiguity, the architect will need an architectural metaphor to define a field of possible analogies and to establish even a vague relationship between the elements of his composition and a series of natural prototypes.

In this way, the architect travels in reverse the road taken by the avant-garde when it transformed the elements of architecture into geometric elements, removing all concrete and institutional features from them. The process of restoring the conventional and linguistic character of

architectural elements inevitably involves the restoration of man as a universal standard and reference. It seems paradoxical that this reintegration does not put us back at all into the blind alley of nineteenth-century eclecticism with its revivals, but into a kind of enchanted garden, in which every ordinary or ancient act seems absolutely new to us. The fact is that not only have historical references changed, but also the way we see and think, and the modern experience rooted within us acts like a slow deformant. Graves' work lets us experience first-hand just how far the "search for lost architecture" takes us, far from a passive revisitation, toward the creative discovery of a "fleeting" memory that paradoxically becomes the only space open to the future. The doll houses Graves builds by taking apart and rebuilding the pieces of an infantile construction are, therefore, an instrument for measuring, an instrument that permits us to measure the increasingly great and unbridgeable distance separating us from the past we seek. And caricature, parody, as Marx said, providentially makes separation less painful.

Michael Graves: *Abrahams House,
Princeton, 1980, study of the façade.*
Michael Graves: *studies for The Portland
Building, Portland (Ore.), 1979—1982.*

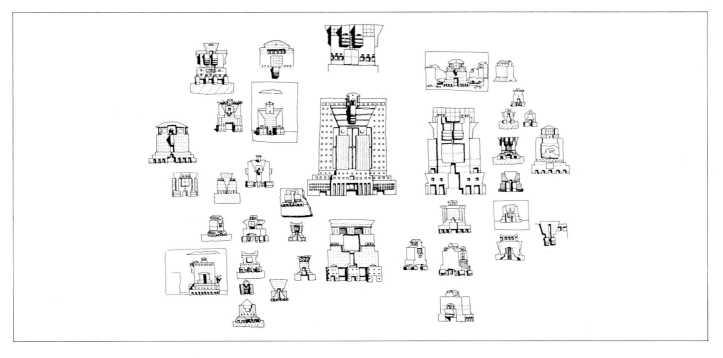

Michael Graves: *Fargo Moorehead Cultural Center Bridge, Fargo (N.D.) and Moorehead (Minn.), 1977–1979, south elevation.*

Michael Graves: *project for a house in Aspen (Col.), 1978, model.*

Thomas Beeby

Thomas Hall Beeby: *Beasely House, Chicago, 1979.*

Thomas Hall Beeby: *"The House of Virgil Built in Expectation of the Return of the Golden Age,"* 1976.   ▷

Thomas Hall Beeby is one of the seven Chicago architects who grouped together a few years ago to assume a role similar to that played in New York by the famous Five, who at the beginning of the seventies opened the way to a detachment from the utopia of the Modern Movement.

Beeby began his career following the noble traditions of the school of Mies, with a glass house set in the landscape like some lunar object, a small glass box similar to those used to imprison precious flowers: an orchid branch, or a rare rose. A Chicago architect of his generation was expected to start out as a follower of Mies van der Rohe. But tough discipline, as we know, produces rejection. Faced with the breakdown of the ideological bases of modernist purism, Beeby reacted by killing his father and finding consolation in the arms of his grandfathers.

Beasley House is the product of this traumatic experience. It is the exact opposite of the glass box, a house in the typical sense of the word, like those drawn by young children, with a pitched roof, a porch, a smoking chimney. The choice of this archetype derives from a critical reflection. The experience of the modern was one of exasperated intellectualism that the general public has never been able to digest. If architects are to resume the dialogue, they must learn to feel at home with those simple ideas about architecture deeply rooted in our imagination and memory.

This new direction derives also from an historical consideration concerning Chicago in particular, and the contradictory role that city played in the Modern Movement. According to Beeby, Louis Sullivan went back to the tradition of the pioneers and farmers, and chose to build "The City of Truth." Burnham, on the other hand, going back to the beginning of the century to the classical language of architecture, proposed the "City of Beauty" as a mirror of the self-control of American civilization. "Mies introduced into the American city an architecture for a transformed European society. He adopted a philosophy that upheld Sullivan's craft position, but used the abstract classical forms of Burnham. This coalition of local attitudes dominated the Chicago architects of the last forty years, but never really satisfied the public.

In recent years, younger architects have opposed the cultural arrogance inherent in Modernism. Ironically, history was desired when Chicago finally acquired a past all its own, after two hundred years of building. The 'City of Truth' and the 'City of Beauty' can finally unite through the inspired use of history and bloom into an American architecture that reflects all the desires of the people."

Beeby's optimistic message derives from a tiring of ideology, from the realization of failures obtained from stretching obedience to intellectualistic norms outside the specific field of architecture. The "inspired use of history" suggested to him a series of drawings of the imaginary, and projects which, once the literal reevocation of the archetype is overcome, tend to draw architecture closer to the sources of dreams, using very simple means still in touch with the Miesian esthetic.

Stanley Tigerman

Five years ago at the exhibition "Europe-America" at the Venice Biennale, Chicago architect Stanley Tigerman, then fifty, presented a project inspired by a kind of erotic obsession. He repeated all the possible combinations of the one-family house, and thus formed a pattern that could be amplified endlessly. An explicit reference to the male organ was easily recognizable in the plan, and the commentary which accompanied the project confirmed the intentional nature of the "quotation" and his "sardonic" intentions with regard to official architectural culture. In the last few years, Tigerman's orientation has changed, although he has not lost his sense of irony. The quality of his work has been enriched by that particular familiar stimulus that derives from a refound dialogue with history. The most telling of his latest projects is in fact a house which he defines "in the manner of the Villa Madama." The building program is not at all monumental: this is a house for a family of five and one housekeeper. There is a series of comfortable facilities ranging from the swimming pool to the tennis court, to the croquet court, to various outdoor environments. This is, therefore, an evident example of the "miniaturization" of the remote Raphaelesque model — one of the poetics with which historical memory is recovered and repressed at the same time, the inevitable ironic connotation of a process that reduces academic models to familiar and ambiguous models, and introduces heroic themes in symbiosis with daily reality. The result of this experiment is quite brilliant, but hardly academic. The spaces derive from the adaptation between the curvilinear exterior profile and the demands of distributing space, using the irregularities of the space to create stimulating situations for the arrangement of furnishings.

Another successful example of miniaturization is the proposal for a supermarket, in which Tigerman cuts out the profile of an ancient street, which he then rebuilds, detached, like a thin screen: a probably unconscious homage to Baudrillard's theory on the quality of the image that derives from a famous line in *Ecclesiastes:* "The image is never that which hides the truth; it is truth which hides what is not true. The image is true."

Stanley Tigerman: *"House in the manner of the Villa Madama,"* 1980, plan.

Stanley Tigerman: *"Animal Crackers,"* Highland Park (Ill.), 1976−1978.

96   Modern architecture produced things without images. The Postmodern begins its journey, favoring images so much that they are separated from objects.

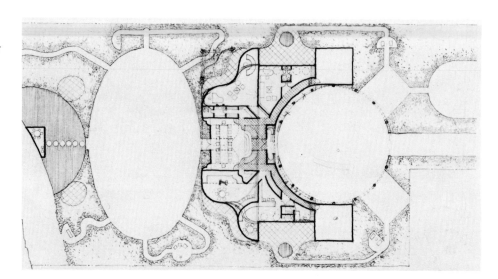

Stanley Tigerman: *project for the*
"Pensacola" residential complex in
Chicago, 1979.

Diana Agrest and Mario Gandelsonas

Diana Agrest, Mario Gandelsonas: *project for a summer house, 1977, elevation and axonometric projection.*
Diana Agrest, Mario Gandelsonas: *apartment house, New York, 1981, elevation.*

98   Diana Agrest and Mario Gandelsonas continue to follow a completely theoretical line of research. They are convinced that architecture still needs a Copernican revolution by which theory as knowledge has the upper hand over the ideology of architecture, which is used to justify adaptation to the needs of social formation and to perpetuate the superstructures of society. Theirs is an austere creed that brings them close to Peter Eisenman, who made this theoretical investigation a way of life. This hardly realistic and quite aristocratic approach has not prevented Agrest and Gandelsonas, one of the great couples on the international architectural scene, from producing projects of high quality in which the recovery of classicism typical of their generation is carried out without artifice, operating on the specific means of architecture without letting the need for theory suffocate the craft of designing with intentions outside architecture. With the project for an apartment house in New York, Agrest-Gandelsonas have left the incubator of theory. They are now involved in building in the city, and they do this with the self-assurance they derive from always having considered the city as a privileged object of their thoughts, the type of scale with respect to which all architecture must be defined in order to contain truth. The building is influenced by the surrounding environment until it involves mimesis, but it is not influenced passively: by interpreting the tower as the missing bell tower of the nearby church, the architects declare polemically that the reasons of the urban fabric must prevail over those of the architectural object. At the same time, they choose to intervene forcefully in that dialogue between forms — consisting of analogies, postponements, contrasts and assonances — which is precisely the urban specific, the collective value of architecture that makes up the structure of the city. The apartment-tower is an homage to the language of places: each of its parts belongs to New York, to its real history and imaginary history, written by architects who have only dreamed of taking part in the city of skyscrapers.

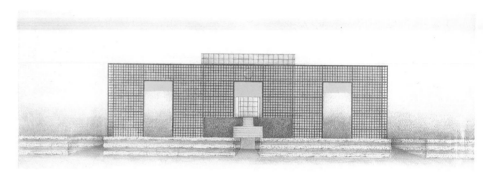

Eugen Kupper

Eugen Kupper: *Nisson House, Bel Air, Los Angeles, 1976–1979.*

100 "Etruscans, Japanese, Celts and Persians have passed under this form... and it still has a precise meaning for us, because it is an archetype." Eugen Kupper, a young California architect, thus justifies his idea of placing a kind of large kiosk, reaching the two eaves of the roof, at the center of the façades of the Washburn house in Oakland. It resembles a kind of dormer that stands above the entire building, giving it an unmistakable identity. In using it, Kupper made the prejudicial choice of a pre-existing motif, of a symbolic form that betrays a "postmodern" attitude. Form comes before function and is chosen not as the automatic result of a process of an analysis of needs, but as an archetype able to reawaken in us a stream of analogies and memories. Someone will ask, "Are all architects becoming platonic?" Lovers of architectural archetypes seem to be influenced less by the platonic theory of innate ideas than by experimental psychology and by the theories formulated by architects like Robert Venturi or Aldo Rossi, who for years have been working on reacquiring some principal foundations that characterize the profession of thinking about and making architecture. More than an innate idea, then, the archetype is a factor in the biological heredity relative to the environment and to its shaping in the service of man. A study of bees, ants or beavers reveals that their biological heredity includes exact notions about how to build a nest, how to regulate temperature and humidity, how to shape the nest to resolve social, defensive, and esthetic problems. Things are not so different for man, even if intelligence and language act upon the elements of biological heredity. It is an incontestable fact that the archetype of the house, and more generally that of the column, the roof, the portal, are all part of the repertoire of conceptual forms of the collective memory. Recently, in a beautiful exhibition in Genoa held on the occasion of a meeting on applied psychology organized by the Turati Club, a series of drawings by children under twelve was shown on the theme "the house I would like to live in." Even if in Italy the majority of the population live in rented barracks and very few, especially in cities like Genoa, have single-family houses, almost all the children drew small houses with sloping roofs and small windows, similar to those that we also drew in our childhood.

The permanence of archetypes in the collective memory of a certain historically and geographically determined group depends on the simplicity and clarity of the form, but also on the intensity of its symbolic signal, on the richness of metaphorical associations it provokes. The abandonment of archetypes proposed by avant-garde culture, and particularly by the Bauhaus (which does not occur, however, in many works of the great masters of this century, from Wright to Mies to Le Corbusier) leads today to the rediscovery of a formidable instrument for communicating through architecture, for reopening a dialogue between architect and inhabitant. The fact remains that, once the archetype is introduced, we must weave around it a story to justify using it again. It is exactly this that Kupper has done so effectively.

Helmut Jahn

Helmut Jahn: *model of the project for a centrally-planned single-family house, 1981.*

Helmut Jahn, barely over forty, is already one of the protagonists of the new architectural culture of Chicago. He entered the office of Murphy Associates in 1967 fresh from Germany, and ten years later became one of its emerging personalities. He is now a partner in the firm. The recognition he received from one of the most important offices in Chicago, a real industry of design, is not surprising, because in just a few years, the quality of his projects relaunched the professional presence of Murphy Associates, and for the first time opened the doors of a hardly negligible channel of publicity: the circuit of the specialized international magazines and commentators of cultural affairs. It is not the first time that an architect of quality has emerged from the large American firms, those massive productive organizations. Generally speaking, a reaction of rejection follows a too personal success, while in this case, an unusual process of identification is taking place.

Friend of Tigerman and Beeby, Jahn serves in the ranks of the postmodern. Those great grave-diggers of the movement who dream of its imminent demise (which they announce every week in a monotonous exorcistic rite) would do well to meditate on the vital impact this produced in the creative parabola of this rising star.

In his work area, which occupies an entire floor of a skyscraper, Jahn had a model made of the Chicago Loop, and placed models of his five or six latest skyscrapers there like an expert juggler, carefully controlling the optic and spatial effect from various viewpoints and the interference with neighboring buildings already finished or under construction. The scene recalls the model of Rome that Alexander VII kept in his bedroom and to which he dedicated long hours of contemplation. Although born in Nuremberg, (or perhaps precisely because of his "Gothic" formation), Jahn dominates the theme of the skyscraper with instinctive confidence and a great capacity for innovation. His skyscrapers have a direction, a privileged orientation, and therefore a façade. They are vertically cut blocks on one side, and shaped with great virtuosity on the other to reflect light and free the ascensional plastic potentialities of the theme. Besides volumes, they are also urban backdrops shaped to favor our

Helmut Jahn: *triangular office building,
Chicago, 1979.*

Helmut Jahn: *model of the project for
"One South Wacker," Chicago, 1979.*

Helmut Jahn: *model of the project for the
Northwest Terminal Building, Chicago,
1979.*

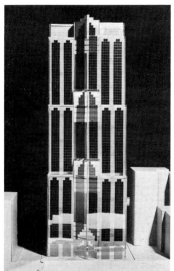

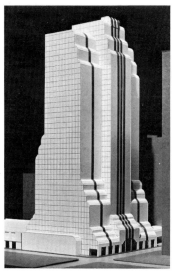

103

Helmut Jahn: *drawing, 1980.*

104   desire to pass through deep urban space visually, and to find indications of movement and penetration on the surfaces that close the building blocks. The entrances, which had been minimized in the Miesian tradition, followed closely in Chicago, are now solid breaks, signs perceptible from a distance, portals in the Romanesque-Gothic sense.

In his office, scattered with models of gigantic buildings worth billions of dollars, there are also models and drawings of a small octagonal house, a paradoxical and unproductive parenthesis for a great office organized for industry, but an indispensable outlet for Helmut Jahn. This small project is a minor opportunity which allows him to go back once again to the dimension of intimacy and delicacy, and to forget for a moment the play of mirrors of the city. The house interprets the laws of the crystallographic growth of the Palladian rotunda, and joyfully expresses the unifying element of Jahn's generation: the nostalgia for a natural order capable of animating the things built by man with the stern beauty of thought and logical construction.

Helmut Jahn: *project for the Chicago Tribune Tower, 1980.*

Helmut Jahn: *drawing, 1980.*

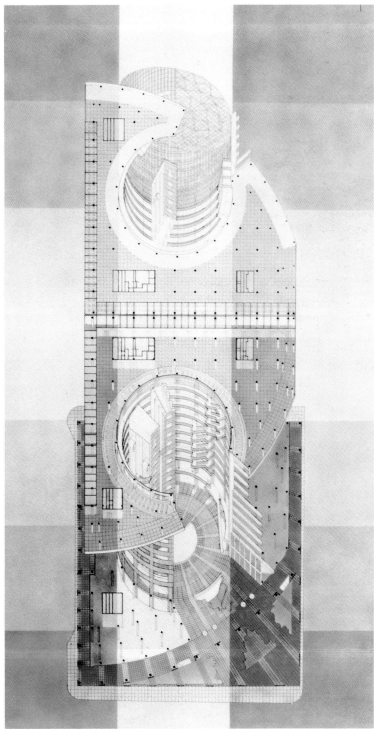

Emilio Ambasz

106 The use of the historical quotation — used
both correctly and incorrectly — is quite
fashionable in architecture, and publishers
with commercial sense have begun to
reprint those significant books that
constituted the indispensable working
instruments of our grandfathers, when
electicism ruled. But the postmodern
quotation insists on a supplement of
creativity to be justified. It has been said
that in order to withdraw the materials he
needs from the bank of history, the
architect must pay interest with his capacity
to reinvent old forms in their new context.
Emilio Ambasz has accomplished this in his
house in Córdoba. This is not surprising,
given the independent and non-conformist
nature of this Argentine architect not yet
forty years old. Like Maldonado and Pelli,
Ambasz is already part of that large group
of Argentine exiles who have assumed
positions of leadership outside their
country. This house recalls a painting by
Magritte, and is almost entirely
underground, and studied specifically for
the climate of Andalusia. The earth
surrounding it guarantees good insulation
and a very particular psychological
situation, somehow related to that of the
houses carved out of tufa by the gypsies of
Guadix. But in contrast to this
disappearance of the built volume, there
rises in one corner of the patio a gigantic
dihedron formed by two white walls, the
two faces of a virtual open cube. In the
convex corner formed by the walls, an
angular wooden balcony — and here is the
literal quotation — finished in a traditional
way, reconstructs one of the fundamentals
of that particular type of language of places
of popular Andalusian architecture. To
arrive at this "removed" lookout, a steep
stairway must be climbed, while there is yet
another one for descending. Ambasz wanted
to recover another feature of Andalusian
architecture influenced by Moorish
tradition: the song of the waters. He thus
designed a small waterfall next to the
stairway, and its sound is gradually
extinguished as one nears his destination.

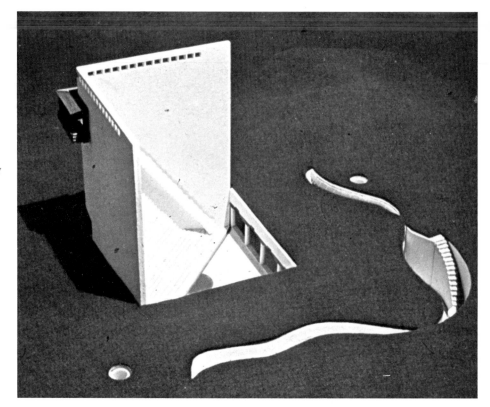

Emilio Ambasz: *house in Córdoba, Spain, 1980, two views of the model.*

Frasca-Zimmer-Consul

108   The skyscrapers of Fountain Plaza in Portland, Oregon are a typical example of a new renewal policy for the central areas of American cities. Now that the tendency to consider tall buildings as a package has passed, in which buildings are prismatic envelopes of a given quantity of offices similar to one another, the metaphor and the imaginary have come back, with the desire to characterize the towers as personalities, and to reflect upon their relationship with their surroundings. The Frasca-Zimmer-Consul group of Portland has designed three buildings together: a central tower housing the Koin Center, a hotel and apartments of twenty-five floors, and a center for offices and stores in a prevalently horizontal building. The tower narrows toward the top, like the skyscrapers of the twenties before the Depression, and its volume is a lively play of light and shadows that play over the horizontal and vertical movements of its profile. The pyramidal pinnacle recalls the Chrysler and Empire State Buildings, but it is conceived not as a sculptural element, but as the logical conclusion of a rigorous system of geometric tapering beginning at the base. There is a fountain in the plaza, but it is the skyscraper that sets itself up as the double of a fountain, as a metaphor of the "frozen fountain," taking up a theme dear to Art Déco culture, launched in the twenties by Claude Bragdon, author of a picture book entitled *The Frozen Fountain* (New York, Alfred A. Knopf, 1924). The protagonist of the book, Simbad, discovers the city of the frozen fountains: "What is this unit-form of nature, the archetype of all visible images? What formula most perfectly expresses our sense of the life-process? Is it not an ascension and a declension — in brief, a fountain: a welling up of a force from some mysterious source, a faltering of the initial impulse by reason of some counter-aspect of that force, a subsidence, a *return* all imagined in the upward rush and downward fall of the waters of a fountain, a skyrocket, a stone flung from the hand into the air? ... The idea once grasped that *life is a fountain*, we see always and everywhere fountains, fountains! — the sun itself, the up-drawn waters and the descending rain, the elm, the willow, the heart, the phallus, and the mammary gland... A building a fountain:

how clarifying a point of view!" Frasca, Zimmer and Consul have given form to Bragdon's intuition, following upon that splendid chapter cut short at the beginning of the thirties, of skyscrapers conversing with the sky. The skyline of American cities is destined to change once again. The Portland group can now be placed next to Cesar Pelli and Helmut Jahn, as experimenters of the urban imaginary, definitively broken off from the obstinate silence of the blocks of Mies van der Rohe.

Frasca-Zimmer-Consul: *fountain, Portland, 1977.*

Houses for Sale

"Houses for Sale:" with this title Leo Castelli presented the demanding public of his New York gallery eight projects for houses done by eight of the most famous architects on the international scene: Emilio Ambasz (Argentina), Peter Eisenman (U.S.A.), Vittorio Gregotti (Italy), Arata Isozaki (Japan), Charles Moore and Cesar Pelli, (U.S.A.), Cedric Price (England), and Oswald Mathias Ungers (Germany). Castelli's thesis is that the market system, which in great part sustains artistic production in the visual arts, is destined to extend successfully into the field of architecture as well. In an earlier exhibition, Castelli had stated that it is possible to sell architectural drawings. He realized, on the contrary, that the unusual character of the merchandise for sale had

to some extent reawakened the sleepy local market of modern art. Now his proposal is one of choosing art galleries as ground for mediation between architect and client. Someone thinking about building a house can go to a gallery and choose a house to his liking, after having examined concrete proposals documented by drawings and models. This initiative was a great success, and constitutes a positive example of the tendency to recognize the great transformations that have taken place before our eyes in the past few years regarding the relationships between art and society, and art and the economic world. Even if the proposed solution is perplexing, the problem is a very real one. The relationship between the architect and his potential clients, once entrusted to the rites

of power and high society, must somehow be democratized, and in this sense every meeting is propitious. The houses presented in the exhibition all seem preoccupied with reawakening in the visitors the memory of an idea, of an ideal model: *On Adam's House in Paradise*, we could say, referring to a successful book by Joseph Rykwert that investigates the archetype of the human dwelling and its historical revisitations. The casuistry of the proposed solutions is quite vast, and goes from the geometric frenzies of Eisenman, to the professional correctness of Price and Gregotti, and from Pelli's exasperated conceptualization to Isozaki's caricature of Palladio. The most convincing attempts are of an opposite sign: Charles Moore's project, charged with allusions and

Cesar Pelli, Arata Isozaki, Oswald Mathias
Ungers: *three projects for the exhibition*
"Houses for Sale."

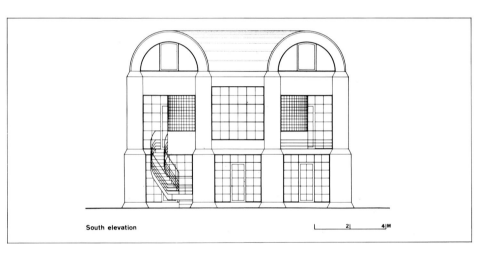

South elevation
2| 4|M

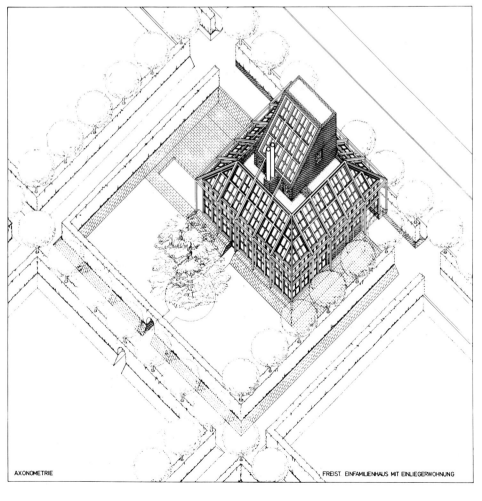

AXONOMETRIE   FREIST. EINFAMILIENHAUS MIT EINLIEGERWOHNUNG

evasions, and the rigorously deductive project by Ungers. Moore, by now an expert in residential organisms interpreted as a tale, conceived his house on an assonance and on a play on words: "Hexastyle, Texas Style." Hexastyles are those temples with six columns on the façade, while Texas is a region of ranches. The house is thus the result of the marriage between the humanistic Italian tradition and the Texas ranch. The concave portico and the monumental stairway derive from Villa Giulia, while the very free organization of spaces comes from the ranch. Under the banner of contamination and irony, there resulted a composition full of charm, capable of giving value and identity to a place that is anything but indeterminate.

More ambitious and therefore more European is Ungers' approach, which imagines three houses inside one another: the matrix a cubic house of stone with small windows, a second house carved out around the first and enclosed by an iron and glass covering, and the third, superimposed on the second, with a second green covering of creepers. The greenhouse effect of the glass enclosure allows for solar heating in winter, and adds the semi-open spaces of the annular garden to the closed interior spaces of the first house; the vegetation of the creeping plants creates an insulating air pocket for summer, when the windows of the greenhouse are taken down to reverse the thermal system from heating to cooling. It is not difficult to find behind Ungers' calligraphy the example of Schinkel, the great neoclassical father of modern Berlin. From Schinkel, he derives the geometric rigor, and from the former's classical ornament comes the manner of designing the creepers as a continuous web that tones down the harshness of the volumes, a pure and reliable way to rediscover the "presence of the past." Ungers' house was one of the first to be sold, I do not remember if to Jacqueline Kennedy or to Liz Taylor. Sign of the inexhaustible seductive force of utopia.

Ridolfi in Terni

Mario Ridolfi: *drawing for a house in Norcia; model for the Hotel Agip in Rome, 1971; project for city office building, Terni, 1981.*

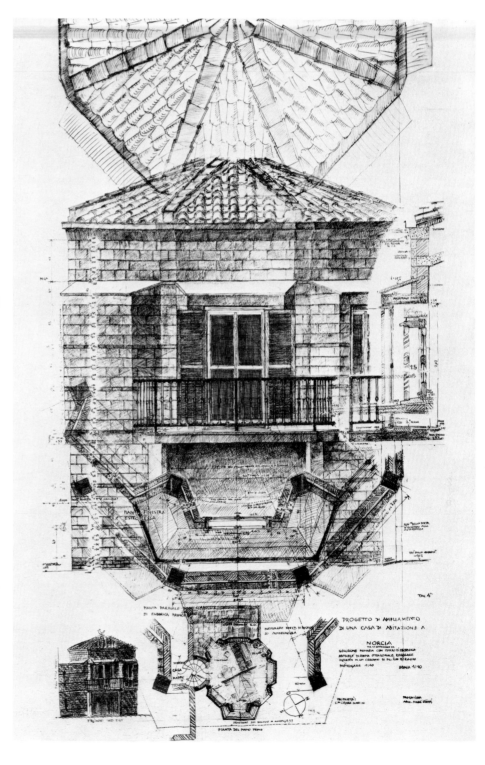

112 Since 1933, when he entered the competition for the master plan of Terni, Mario Ridolfi has been involved with that city. For almost fifty years, he has dedicated to the city of Terni the same love and attention that Palladio dedicated to Vicenza and Sanmicheli to Verona. Under very different conditions much less favorable to architecture, Ridolfi has repeated the miracle of the identification between an architect and the face of a city that is one of the great attractions of urban Italy. It was above all after the Second World War, however, with the reconstruction plan of 1948, and the master plan of 1960, and with the innumerable buildings put up by him and by his followers, that the Ridolfi-Terni relationship began to be a determining force, even if the old fountain realized with Cagli in 1939 signals the happy beginnings of this "marriage of love."

The plan for Terni is an isolated example of urbanism that is above all "design of the city." By virtue of the timely launching of detailed plans, this plan avoids the equivocations and negative displays of the urbanism of zoning and sociological analysis, so seemingly rigorous, but really incapable of being translated into practical indications and cultural choices. Using a criterion that seemed outdated twenty years ago, but which today seems advanced, Ridolfi has used the plan to define precisely and flexibly what could be called the urban shell, or that continuous spatial quantity defined through the quality of the built architecture. Considering the space of the streets and piazzas as a sort of waterway, Ridolfi conceived of the embankments that contain it, assigning to the architects the task of giving form to these backdrops within which the daily drama of urban life unfolds. Fortunately, many of these backdrops were designed by Ridolfi himself. Particularly successful is Corso del Popolo, the artery that has given new and original order to the "demolition" brutally carried out in the historic center by the bombardments of the last war. Acting as the good surgeon of the city (Ridolfi would probably prefer to consider himself a country doctor, but the seriousness of the wounds required highly specialized interventions), the architect thought out into all its parts that whole of cuts,

additions, and sewing up that could have 113
healed up the wound and given a new heart
to the city.

If Corso del Popolo was the only real urban
street built in post-war Italy, Ridolfi is now
trying, after having enriched the city in the
sixties with the Pallotta and Franconi
houses, to realize a modern protagonist: a
tower for city offices, inserted in the center
of a wider void, will lead the fascinating
sequence of old and new to a harmonious
balance, the distinctive sign of this great
planning effort. The city office building —
without which the whole work seemed
truncated and incomplete — develops the
theme of the tower, especially dear to
Ridolfi since his youth, when he imagined
the fantastic tower for restaurants shaped
like a twisted column. The great hexagonal
volume resembles that of a baptistry, and it
is most suitable for contrast with the
prismatic blocks of the neighboring
buildings, calling attention to the dynamic
value of the space of the street. Realized
with that extraordinary capacity to
dominate detail and make it "sing," this
work will honor a well administered city
that has succeeded in renewing, on an
urbanistic level, the glories of the major
cities of our Renaissance.

Massimo Scolari

Massimo Scolari: *façade drawings for the Strada Novissima, 1980.*

114   Scolari's beautiful watercolors that have appeared in the international architecture magazines of the past few years leave one curious and somehow unsatisfied, because they seem to be fragments of a long imaginary tale separated from their context, tesserae of a mosaic, or pieces of a "jigsaw puzzle" like those given to children to stimulate their sense of order and unity. The pieces we possessed were always too few to let us successfully recompose the entire image: the idea of the city and of architecture that Scolari has slowly constructed with his industrious hands. Now, a precious book aids us in reconstructing his imaginary world: a text published in Florence and containing almost all of Scolari's production in chronological order, put together with passion and philological detachment by Francesco Moschini. The book is a trip into the imaginary, but the memory that remains after having made this journey is not vague and indefinable, as after a dream, but crystal clear, almost as if we could minutely perceive its every aspect, tracing its marvelous itinerary. The truth is that Scolari is an architect: he wears the clothes of the painter very expertly, but does not give up "having compasses in his eyes," in the words of Leonardo, that reduce appearance to size, impression to description. Seeing all his crystalline works together, we might ask ourselves what kind of world he lives in, and the nature of his relationship with our own daily world. The answer can be only this: his is an image scrupulously faithful to this world, operated by selection, excluding relentlessly, and choosing amid the immensity of the insignificant that tiny bit that counts. Moschini speaks correctly of "censure:" Scolari censures the world and presents an amended version to us; he censures the worldly vanities of architecture and gives it back to us as a skeleton, as an idea; he censures the perspective vision with its materialized points of escape and re-presents it as an axonometric projection, as an impersonal representation in which the object maintains its autonomy and is not subject to the laws of the human body. Because of this, Scolari is very important to the architecture being created all over the world, which is no longer modern, but neither ancient nor antique, an architecture

Massimo Scolari: *painted architecture.*

constantly searching for archetypes, for
consistent ideas, for effects of removal, and
which takes off from the annulment of a
code. With respect to the conciseness of the
"exclusivists" and the "inclusivists,"
Scolari has no doubts: he is convinced, like
Montale, that "This only we can tell you
today, what we are *not*, and what we do *not*
want."

G.R.A.U.

G.R.A.U. is a group of fourteen Roman
architects who have been working under
this name since 1964. In the Strada
Novissima in Venice, the group ironically
gathered behind the façade of a Roman
columbarium its own *opera omnia*,
consisting of hundreds of beautiful
drawings. G.R.A.U. has offered the most
paradoxical and exact definition of itself,
proposing to be "the mysterious object of
the present figurative panorama." In effect,
this group (which has remained compact,
even if individual personalities have begun
to emerge) has passed through the phases of
the architectural debate and holds one of
the most advanced positions on the
postmodern scene, since it anticipated many
of its theses and contradictions, and has
overcome them through a particularly
significant effort at self-criticism. This
mature and evident position, recognized by
this time internationally, is still completely
ignored in Italy, where, carefully kept away
from the university and from positions of
power, the members of G.R.A.U. continue
to carry out a semi-clandestine activity.
Even though they recently won the
competition for the flower market of
Sanremo, and presented a final project
that, in my view, is among the best things
produced in Italy in the last twenty years,
the commission was rescinded, thus
depriving that Ligurian city of a rare
occasion to redeem the ignoble urbanistic
policy adopted after the war, which
transformed Sanremo from a pearl of the
Riviera into a free-for-all fair of reinforced
concrete. Not even the commissioner
Nicolini, who had recognized their role, in
a book he wrote in 1971, has remembered
their troublesome presence. Even today, in
order to see some of their works, it is
necessary to travel beyond the furthest
outskirts of Rome, and search for them in
small towns where they constitute
"diamonds in a haystack." Since the end of
last year, however, one very significant
work (even if it consists only of large
colored panels of enameled steel) can be
found in Paris, in the new town of
Marne-la-Vallée in a residential complex
designed by Henri Ciriani. One panel, six
by seven meters, and the other, one meter
twenty by eighty centimeters, designed by
Sandro Anselmi and Franco Pierluisi,
belong to a world of the image that holds a

dialogue with the two principal factors of
G.R.A.U.'s research, classicism and
popular art, understood as reconcilable
polarities.

The instrument of perspective, recovered
and renewed through drawing and painting,
becomes the basis for a rethinking of the
architectural heredity of the West, a
comparison between how much is still valid
of the lesson of the Modern Movement, and

how much of the notion of classicism
remains a common and inalienable
patrimony of our civilization. G.R.A.U.'s
panels were shown at Cinecittà before they
were brought to Paris, and they were
viewed enthusiastically by the initiates who
were able to see them thanks to Francesco
Moschini. Is it possible that Roman culture,
so poor in resources, continues to waste its
best energies?

G.R.A.U.: *project for the flower market,*
Sanremo, plan and view of the roof.

Roberto Gabetti and Aimaro d'Isola

Roberto Gabetti, Aimaro d'Isola: *house, Pino Torinese, 1967.*

118 Roberto Gabetti and Aimaro Oreglia d'Isola were already Postmodern in 1954, when they built their Bottega d'Erasmo in Turin in the shadow of the Mole Antonelliana, on one of the many straight streets with no particular identity that form the urban fabric of this very regular city, that has the appearance of being almost colonial. They were already Postmodern, since they had spontaneously abandoned the modernist orthodoxy of white superimposed boxes. Curiously and ironically, they revisited the premodern, the unhappy childhood and rebellious adolescence of the Modern Movement, which then landed on the bureaucratic shoals of the International Style. They revisited the premodern, the style of the pioneers and experimenters, probably attracted to this first phase of modernity by the not yet lost capacity to have a dialogue with places and their traditions. Both of them had Turin and Piedmont in their blood as much as Pavese did, and they realized that being local is one of the best ways to become international, because the most universal things in architecture, from Brunelleschi to Wright, are those with the strongest roots in their place of origin. Roberto and Aimaro, leaders of neo-Liberty, were thus accused of proposing an "infantile regression" of Italian architecture, while they were actually prefiguring a crisis which would become clear only twenty years later, and whose results still must be defined and clarified.

In order to understand where to land the ship of Postmodernism, by now full of opportunists and last-minute converts, searching perhaps for new, more reassuring labels, we should analyze their work. After abandoning their paradoxical tones, they have concentrated on the architecture-nature relationship and cautiously use historical memory to enrich their built images with a deep resonance. The residential hotel Gabetti and d'Isola built in Sestrière finally realizes an idea they had in a competition in 1973, and is particularly suited to the strong slope of the land. The body of the building, developed horizontally along the curving slope, does not detach itself from the ground like a fragile lamella, but leans against the slope and becomes the equivalent of an emerging rock step, or an earthen barrier that

mirrors precisely the physical environment. As in the apartment block in Ivrea, a great semi-interred crescent, the most direct reference is to the crescents of the thermal city of Bath, masterpiece of the urban culture of Georgian England. But in the detail of the glass sheds, one is also reminded of the Baroque cornices of certain Piedmontese buildings like Santa Marta in Agliè, where classical matrices join with the complexity of natural forms.

Gabetti and d'Isola have written: "We have always worked in Turin or in Piedmont, habitat, hunting ground, den of a large dragon that leaves traces, signs of his meals and sleep around the entire region: his back is made of sheds; he leans against high and low glass buildings for a den; he has many antennae, and long tails made of highways. It is impossible to ignore him: living and working here means always feeling his presence, it means living with and gauging oneself by the laws of the dragon. Someone tried to tame him, others tried to chain him down, and still others have adopted him as their 'mother.' Many people are convinced that they themselves are the dragon: some are his brain, his teeth, others... Some goad him with long lances: to wake him up? to wound him? We will be asked: what are we doing, what have we done with our little pencils?" To the architects' self-questioning, we could respond that the dragon's den has become his very skin, and that it is no easy task to maintain its design and identity.

Roberto Gabetti, Aimaro d'Isola:
residential hotel, Sestrière, 1981.

Guido Canella

Guido Canella and others: *residential complex in Bollate, 1974, general plan, elevation, plan, views.*

120 Of all the masters of the third generation of Italian architects, all fifty or older, Guido Canella is one of the most active and problematic. His colleague Rossi has attained broad consensus, especially among the young, and seems intent on renewing his architectural vocabulary in depth. Gregotti seems to have resigned himself to the more practical aspects of the field, and Gabetti and Valle continue to work a bit aloofly. Canella's course, on the other hand, is difficult and intense, and always animated by a sense of doubt. He tends not to mediate between and document the contradictions of the cultural debate, but rather to represent them, quite evidently, with a kind of "violence of the image" that has nothing to do with the gratuitous urban disorder generally found in the outskirts of large cities. In his case, violence arises not from a play of random forms justified only by the variety of functions, but from a coherent attempt to restore a symbolic role to buildings, and to make them into talking personalities amid the mute anonymity of the urban mass.

The architect demonstrates his expertise in working on a large scale in the residential complex outside Milan in Bollate, in three- and six-storey buildings with exterior hallways. His ability to intelligently confront the collective aspects of the residential theme is also evident here. With respect to his previous experiences in Segrate and Pieve Emanuele, he continues his investigation, letting the archetypal forms of the classical tradition, and the pediment in particular, reemerge as the symbolic keys to the building. But the study of complexity, the plurality of architectural languages, is drastically reduced, almost as if the architect wanted to pass from the clamor of a Wagnerian orchestra to a more contained group of strings. His compositional process gains in clarity and communicability, and like the cinematographic technique of crossed fade-out, tends to make a second image appear behind the real image. In this case, the second one never really comes to the surface, but is hidden like a barely decipherable watermark.

The real image here is the temple, almost as if the house, prototype in turn of the temple, could rediscover its identity only by regaining that maximum degree of typicality

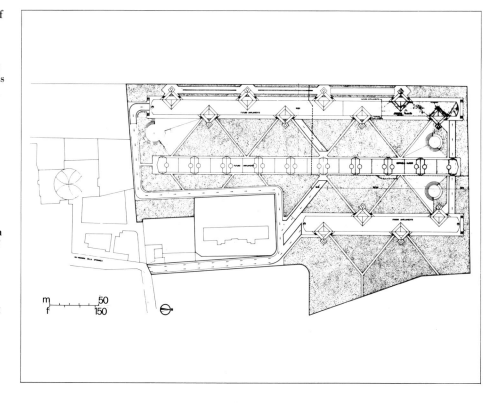

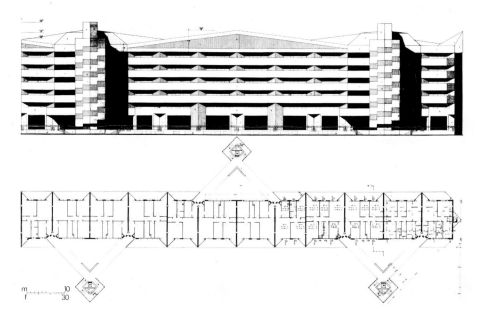

that once served as the model of every
temple of all civilizations from Japan to
Greece. The pediments are very evident
above the volumes of the houses, but in a
transparent version made variable by the
light filtering through the grilles. The
columns, on the other hand, appear and
disappear according to light, position and
point of view. In the three-storey houses,
diagonal towers separate the repeated units,
aligned like the façades of a Renaissance
street.

Sandro Anselmi

A cemetery and a slaughterhouse in Santa Severina, a small town in Calabria: these are the latest works by Sandro Anselmi, the leader of G.R.A.U., and one of the most talented Roman architects of the latest generations.

Faced with the indifference and hostility of those in power in the city (even in leftist city councils), good architects are left with only the rural exile of towns, where an enlightened mayor or commissioner proves that architecture can be recovered as an instrument of education and good government.

The two works in Santa Severina, soon to be joined by the reorganization of the main piazza, show the effects of Anselmi's "Roman" sensibility. They are classical works in the best sense of this term, so mistreated and corrupted by bad use.

The meaning of "classical" must be agreed upon. Either it refers to the academic conventions that attempted to codify and embalm the heredity of the ancient world, connecting it to an idea of formalistic perfection and bureaucratic absoluteness, in which case a good number of Greek and Roman buildings are not classical, or are actually "anti-classical;" or, more reasonably, the current use of the concept is considered correct, and the "classical" is interpreted historically. In this case, the adjective is surprisingly up-to-date, because it singles out what is logical and natural in architecture, or what produces consensus since it avails itself of deeply-rooted conventions tied to simple and concrete ideas.

The "classical" can thus be free and imaginative because it is "ordered:" in short, the contrary of the present chaos brought on by the illusion of escaping from all forms of control.

Anselmi's works have that particular type of complexity proper to classical works, a complexity deriving from a great wealth of relationships between the parts of the building.

These parts are not mechanically juxtaposed for simple coupling or superimposition, but seem to originate and develop together, each one working to determine the form and position of the other.

It is clear why the ancients spoke of architecture as "imitation of nature." In the small cemetery, each part has a symbolic value, and the conventional forms that designate the grave are reviewed, numbered, and described to bring out their potential for expression and communication.

Like magnetic poles, the two little temples on either side of the entrance create an architectural field where the visitor is trapped into receiving the message of an architecture in which time and memory are the image.

The cylindrical slaughterhouse with its cubic lantern defines a separate place just as clearly: a hidden function in which society confronts nature and death through the cold neutrality of institutions.

Sandro Anselmi: *slaughterhouse, Santa Severina, 1981.*

Sandro Anselmi: *studies for the cemetery, Santa Severina, 1981.*

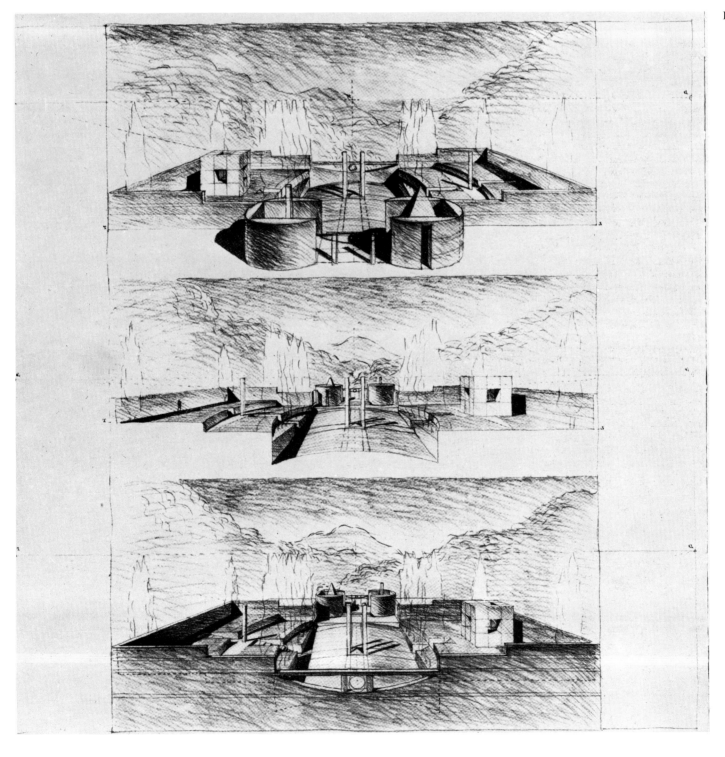

Franco Purini

124 With the pharmacist's house in Gibellina, Franco Purini and Laura Thermes definitively come out from that kind of hiding, informing the field of "drawn architecture," or better, of "well-drawn architecture," that will remain one of the historical features of the investigations of the seventies. Their work certainly is not wanting in notoriety. Purini's name has already entered into the history of architecture, and rightly so. But his architecture, populating the pages of journals and books like ghosts, had never before been part of the body of the city, except for some temporary construction. The pharmacist's house in Gibellina, however, is already under construction. It will soon become one of the few attractions in this town destroyed by an earthquake and rebuilt, often by illustrious names, in the style of the most empty and wretched modernity. Like many of Purini's creations, the house of the pharmacist has a face, it is indeed a character that "describes itself" not without satisfaction, and tells a story of its own, aspiring to restore identity to an empty urban landscape.

Laura Thermes relates that the commission was obtained while she was conducting research during the seminars in Gibilmanna on the urbanistic results of the reconstruction of Gibellina. Her investigation was quite disheartening, and focused on the chaotic nature of the urban fabric which grew on a network of streets whose "rationality," entrusted exclusively to the instrument of analysis, could be seen in plan, but had been completely destroyed in spatial and visual reality.

There is only one possible remedy for this undifferentiated panorama, where it is difficult to find one's bearings: a "talking architecture" capable of expressing a place in its deepest essence, its recognizability, its potential familiarity. Despite their ties with the simplifying morphology of rationalism, Purini and Thermes understand this problem, since they are already outside the equivocations of neorationalism, and do not believe in architecture without images. The house stands at the intersection of two streets, like a sign that makes its entire surroundings recognizable. In its evident symbolism, it seems to want to express, with loving irony, the importance of the pharmacy as a place delegated with the

Franco Purini: *two theoretical drawings.*

civilization of towns, certainly changed but still tied to certain themes of its recent history that have had a significant literary tradition in the course of this century.

On one of the façades there appears, like a clearly printed ideogram, the archetype of the house, with its sloping roof in forms similar to those used in the Strada Novissima in Venice. A proof, as if it were needed, that the Strada Novissima was not the project of a real street, but a street of streets, a symbol of a culture that is using both new and very old means to reacquire the space of the city.

Franco Purini, Laura Thermes:
pharmacist's house in Gibellina, 1981,
drawings of the façades.

Roberto Pirzio Biroli

Roberto Pirzio Biroli, the young architect who designed the reconstruction of the town hall of Venzone, came to the fore during the student movement of the sixties. To meet him, a bit dreamy but overwhelming in his rapid-fire speech, seething with ideas and plans, is like going back to the time of Valle Giulia with its endless student assemblies and great hopes.

The experience of the student movement, however, did not cause frustration and anger in this case, but gave rise to a desire to face reality — even if instead of changing the entire world immediately, just a small piece of land is changed, walls are patiently put up, and a shelter is made, a symbol of the desire to regain a dear lost space.

The disasters of Irpinia, Belice, and Friuli occurred within very few years of one another, but these were very important years for architecture, and this can be seen in the change in tone of many of the projects. The tragedy in Belice happened in a period of ephemeral comeback of modernist utopias, and the reconstruction of that zone seriously felt the effects of this: mastodontic infrastructures, buildings similar to those of the urban periphery, proud of their alienation from the landscape and from the destroyed towns, with a total absence of any reference to memory; a pile of meteorites fallen randomly from above, and more often than not remaining on paper to embellish the pages of specialized magazines. In Friuli, however, the winds have changed. In that region, the last residues of this "culture of violence to the environment" can now be seen along with the positive results of a radical criticism of the Modern Movement. In Venzone, Pirzio Biroli rebuilt the town hall and the entire hamlet of Portis, which was moved for geological reasons one kilometer north after long and suffered hesitations. The town hall derives from an impassioned and elegant rereading of local archetypes reproposed through the filter of a technology suited to a seismic area and to the organization of a modern building site. The straight volume, well-shaped by the projection of the roof, discreetly punched out and adding tension to the masonry wall, stands out boldly against the background of the mountains like a Palladian building, in a manner that has become typical of the Veneto region. Continuing the analogy, the

128   architect used a row of small square windows beneath the cornice to recover the rhythm of the corbels of the typical entablatures of the region. But there is one element in particular that gives character to the entire building, carrying even further this play of historical references: the large central window, a quotation from Palladio whose serial rhythm and technological interpretation also relate it to Schinkel and Viollet-le-Duc. Pirzio Biroli uses the theme of the large window very cleverly, both to mediate the connection between the building and the ground, and to suggest, through projecting volumes, a more immediate reading of the cement network.

In the hamlet of Portis, the work of Pirzio Biroli and his collaborators was carried out in constant contact with the inhabitants of the old destroyed village, who set up a cooperative. These people not only helped with defining the building program according to their practical needs, but also influenced the esthetic choices, insisting on keeping alive the memory of the village without parody or direct imitation. The architects worked on types, on structures part of the local tradition, on the evidence of the material culture that exists in symbiosis with our bodies. Their work was checked each day through meetings and visits to the building site, where the townspeople themselves worked, renewing an ancient tradition.

Venzone will thus be the first Italian town to have a "postmodern" town hall, but not because it was inspired by the most current and ephemeral New York fashions, but because it realizes that we are now part of the postindustrial society freed from the myths of the avant-garde. It is a society which needs to experiment new means of production, a society in which architecture is no longer used to save the world and teach people how to live, but only to perpetuate the rules of a task that is almost as old as man, and to make possible new alliances between man and the places of his life.

Aurelio Cortesi

Aurelio Cortesi, Paolo Zermani: *project for the new city of Pallavicina, 1981.*

Bernardo Bertolucci decided to shoot part of his latest film in a house in Langhirano built several years ago by Aurelio Cortesi, halfway up a hill near the castle of Torchiara. Bertolucci has been accused of insisting too often on his Parmesan roots, of being too ready to include bits of dialect and local color like the famous "culatello" in his films. It is no wonder, then, that he chose a house like that by Cortesi, tied inseparably to the place, as if it had been created from a knot of memories, uninterrupted frequenting of deep passions for certain materials and forms that make up the identity of a particular place. The comparison with food and dialect is very apt for explaining the utopias, violences and disappointments of the last fifty years of architecture.

At the end of the twenties, the "Functionalist Statute" spread throughout the world, introducing a series of rules that reduced the language of architecture to one of Euclidean geometry (cubes, cubes and more cubes, some pyramids, a few cones and very few spheres). A strict prohibition was established which outlawed the use of already existing architectonic forms, and especially those typical of different parts of the world. If we were to make a comparison between architecture and food, we could say that the advent of the International Style established something similar to what would happen if all traditional foods were suddenly prohibited, local specialties that constitute the pride of each place, and substituted with industrially produced pills manufactured with the correct amount of substances necessary for survival. If something like this had actually happened with food, resistance would certainly have reversed the prohibitions. But architecture touches our tastes and interests less directly, and except for some reservations and evasions, this architectural prohibition lasted at least forty years.

The house in Langhirano is a good example of a return to the place and its flavor that began in Italy in the fifties, and which has produced our finest works of architecture. Like a dowser, Cortesi senses the proximity of the farmhouses of the plain, of the military constructions that are perhaps the most characteristic elements of the Emilian landscape, especially the castle of Torchiara, "created with such perfection of

beauty," wrote Bonaventura Angeli in 1591, "that nothing more could be desired. The passerby sees the pleasing arches, the lovely towers, the graceful little houses, and charming loggias." The modern house has stone walls, steep steps, window splays that echo vents, and a roof raised on small pilasters that recalls the great roofs raised on the battlements of ancient castles,

beginning with Francesco di Giorgio. The tone of the building is neither academic nor hostile. The reference to fortification is a metaphor used to enrich the image with connotations and immediately deny them, letting the rites and needs of daily life extract from the solemn structure a varied and unpredictable story, told with the cordial tones of the lovely Emilian dialect.

Aurelio Cortesi: *house in Langhirano,*
1972.

Ordinary Architecture

Architect unknown: *house in San Rufo (Salerno), 1980.*

In the Anglo-Saxon world, the word "contextualism" would be used, more suitable than the word "ambientamento" in Italian. The small single-family house built by an unknown architect most likely for his personal use, on the road leading to Selinunte, is an obvious example of a tendency widespread the world over throughout history: the tendency to imitate, to replicate *in loco*, to repeat, even in miniature, a famous model in an area where its visual presence has psychological weight. In architecture, imitation is a precious principle (unjustly scorned in the name of originality at all costs by those who know neither how to invent, nor to copy correctly) connected directly to the beauty of many urban environments in which a certain type of façade and organism are repeated with small variations to form a coherent whole. Many Italian streets and piazzas are like sonnets, in which, instead of a series of hendecasyllables, there is a series of "façades" of the same width, the same number of windows, varying only with regard to decorative forms or the height of the floors. The anonymous builder from Selinunte, wanting a small house with a garden, did well to replicate as a distinctive element a temple portico with a small living space inside. The house has four Doric columns crowned by a pediment, and is built in concrete with some degree of freedom in the proportions of the members of the order. This is a piece of architecture that recalls the ironic use of archetypes begun by Robert Venturi, and that demonstrates the vitality and courage of what could be called ordinary architecture, architecture built by "minor" technicians outside the cultured area of officially recognized architectural currents.
Italian everyday architecture, widespread especially in the South, but also in Emilia and Latium, is a completely ignored chapter that deserves more attention. Until now, only photographers who exercise the profession of ironic reflection have noticed it. This is a chapter in which a creativity free of complexes is affirmed, mixing ancient and modern fragments with supreme indifference. What moves it and makes it develop along diverging roads is the wish to symbolize pride, restlessness, pleasure, the desire for a house, the social level one belongs to and even one's own

132   geographic area and its corresponding
ethnic traditions.
In spite of those who believe in the rigid
divisions between creators and consumers,
between inventors and followers, a
recognition of self-built architecture could
demonstrate that there is more imagination
in the ordinary than in the cultured. Even
if one does not subscribe to this superiority
of the naïve, it can be stated that
everything is now changing, even in the
most remote cultural periphery.

Sandro Mendini

Sandro Mendini's strength is expressed entirely in his ingratiating frailty as a timid but determined boy, determined above all never to grow up, to create a scandal whenever possible, to find an irreverent way out of every cultural situation. He is as delicate and small as is necessary to give emphasis to his big, lively eyes with their embarassing, questioning gaze. Mendini assumed direction of *Casabella*, once the great magazine of Persico and Pagano, which became a boring bulletin managed by a non-existent cultural right-wing after the dismissal of Rogers. An unexpected vitality was restored to the magazine, which in Mendini's hands became the mouthpiece of the most current trends of the so-called "radical" avant-garde. Then, when the new owners of *Casabella* deemed it worthy of a different shining future, Mendini founded *Modo*, one of the few new publishing experiments in the field of design, the first courageous attempt to overcome the anemic ideology of design, preserved in mothballs by the cartels of Milanese industry. Now, having inherited *Domus* from his exact opposite the great Gio Ponti, man of faith and fervid building activity, the skeptical Mendini has restored prestige and vivacity to that magazine, making it one of the few territories open to architectural culture whose foolish sectarianism has been replaced by irony, by the joy of contrast, by the pleasure of finding people together in the same room who had stopped talking to one another long ago.

Mendini's creative side is particularly evident in his capacity to "make magazines," to create explosive mixtures of contrasting things, astutely managing a well calculated impartiality. Another side of Mendini's creativity is demonstrated by his old incursions into the superephemeral kingdom of "poor" architecture, and by his industrially produced objects, delicate and awkward, but endowed with an immediate attraction like characters in a children's story. Most recently Mendini has produced a series of exhibition-performances that renew the splendors of the Futurist performances in an "integrated" climate, where even scandal has become part of the repertoire. Less convincing, or better, completely literary, is the "infinite piece of furniture" that tries to make us relive, in a sweet and delirious dream, the still too

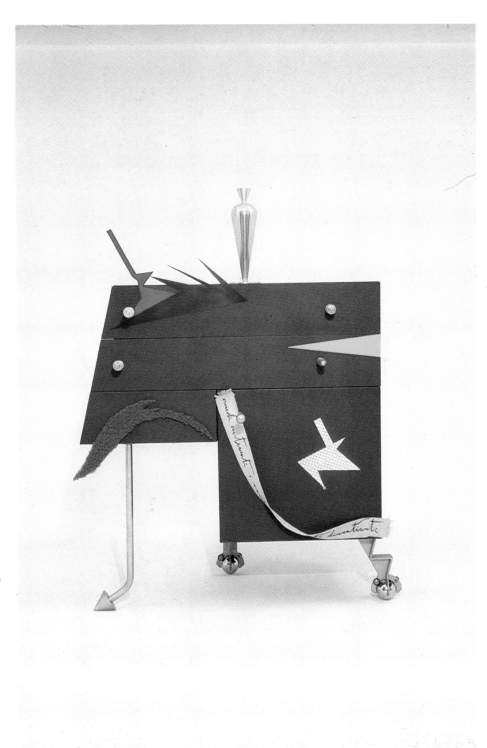

134 recent delights of popular design of the fifties. More successful is his performance of hermaphrodite architecture, a half-hour presentation in the Pavilion of Contemporary Arts in Milan.

"In its millennial development," writes Mendini, "the architectural discipline is a heroic series of male myths, of convex and affirmative forms, at whose center the female Penelope digs out, with a different attitude, the identity of her dwelling and its often unseen parameters. But where should those architectonic subtleties be placed that are lost in the night of time, those sensations given to us even in the past that we need so desperately, the deadened sounds, the twilights, the smells, the memories, the fabrics, scrolls, caresses, fluids, hiding places, the flowers, the grilles, cobwebs, pink colors, the tiny things, glass bells, the microenvironmental involvements? Has this not always been a project of hermaphrodite nature?...
Hermaphroditus, son of Hermes and Aphrodite, taking part in both the masculine and feminine nature in a single delicate, languid and beautiful body: a nymph falls in love with him, and his body coalesces with hers. Hermaphroditus is that 'project and its opposite,' of architecture and décor together, arising from masculine and feminine desires. In every man there is a latent woman, in every woman a latent man, in a continuous breathless search, in perennial conflict: could it be that a similar specular and hybrid architect is the designer of the future 'hovels' of our human race immersed in the cosmic fear of the postmodern world?"

Hermaphrodite architecture consisted of a coffer inspired by the archetype of the house, whose interior was scattered with a series of oval openings connected by classical festoons. In each of the ovals, a real mouth could be seen, belonging to a person hidden in the wall cavity. Whatever the label used to classify it, this experiment derives its effectiveness from the use of architectural figuration, from a reference to architectural institutions, and perhaps signals the end of sterile modernist inhibitions in Mendini's career.

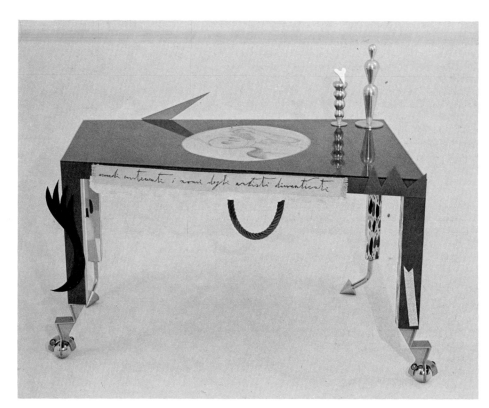

Fernando Montes

Fernando Montes: *project for a housing complex in Cergy Pontoise, 1978, drawings.*

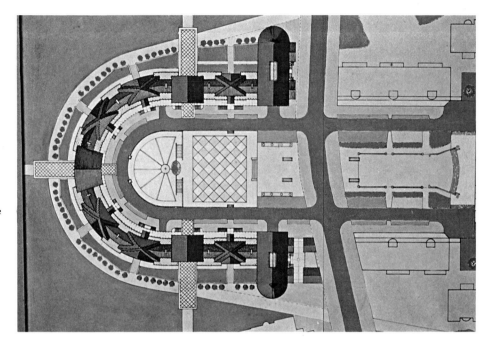

Fernando Montes, born in 1941, has abandoned his political extremism of the beginning of the seventies for a coherent investigation of elementary assemblages of forms that seem "already seen," familiar. Classicism is his guiding idea, an unexpected classicism that cannot be reduced to a style: a classicism revealed in the balance, in the relationship between the various objects next to one another or superimposed, an always complementary relationship of reciprocal desires. In this universe of forms, large and small things, fundamental or accessory, are all indispensable. The obelisk, the spire, the small window are not "ornaments," because their "weight" is necessary to balance the scales, to make negative forces equal to positive ones. Montes landed in France from his country across the ocean with the intention of finding one of the fixed places of great architecture. Disappointed by the poverty of the present, he did not hesitate to look for his masters in another time, in the "revolutionary" tradition, where the kingdom of reason affirms its permanent and abstract laws. Last year at the Venice Biennale, Montes presented a project for a semiology institute dedicated to Roland Barthes, in which Palladio and Ledoux join hands, and seem to want to involve Aldo Rossi and Leon Krier in the celebration of archetypes. The intellectual game, played with an open hand, prevails over the investigation of a real space. On other occasions, Montes has shown that he knows how to get down from the stage of symbolic design without tripping, to involve himself in actual production.

This is the case of the housing complex in Cergy Pontoise, a large circular piazza rimmed by houses crossed with large arched openings, one of the most successful applications of the idea of the great urban court, reproposing the theme of the Palais Royal in new terms. For the problem of Les Halles, Montes is one of the few architects who gave much importance to the presence of the church of St. Eustache, placing it in the background of a U-shaped space open toward the side of the sixteenth-century building. This is a solution with a dialogue, based on a play of correspondences between old and new parts of the city.

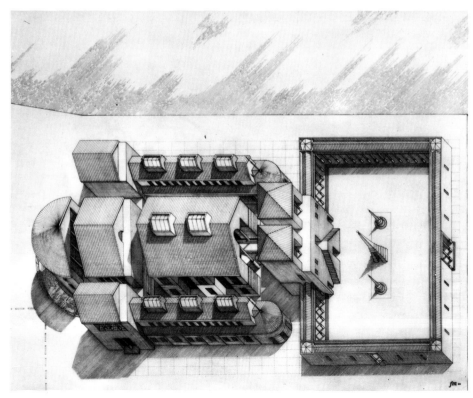

Fernando Montes: *project for a housing complex, 1981.*
Fernando Montes: *project for a housing complex, 1981.*

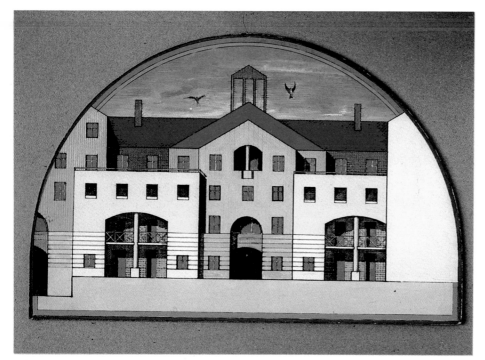

Ricardo Porro

A short distance from the source of the Rhine where the gold of the Niebelungen was hidden, lies Vaduz, the capital of Liechtenstein, which has become one of the golden meccas of international capital. Its tolerant laws have attracted legions of financiers and owners of ghost-companies in search of privileges and fiscal evasion. For some time now, visitors to the city have been attracted not only by its lovely landscape, but by the presence of a disconcerting building sitting on a green slope. From afar, the building recalls the forms of a large fist entangled in a cascade of gilded pipes. Local opinion, which had no problems in digesting the worst creations of the ascetic International Style, rose up a while ago against this anticonformist fist, and succeeded, through certain details — the mobility of the hanging lamellae and the presence of verbal captions — in preventing the Cuban architect Ricardo Porro from realizing his idea completely, the first project he built in Europe after leaving Cuba in 1966.

Porro personally experienced the Cuban revolution and came out of it uninhibited, freed from what he had learned about architecture in school. His friendship with Fidel Castro during the Revolution led to Porro's obtaining the commission to build the National School of Plastic Arts in Havana, which after fifteen years can still be considered one of the few original attempts to found a popular language of architecture for the new needs of a Socialist society. The art school — part of a program intended to attract young people to Cuba from every part of Latin America, thus creating a center of revolutionary training — lucidly interprets in architectural terms Afro-Cuban culture, which had so much influence in the formation of modern popular music. It takes inspiration from the archetypal forms of the villages of African huts and the Baroque domes of the Hispanic-American tradition. But it has a provocatory and disturbing side in the presence of an erotic symbolism immediately evident to the observer. The general layout, with its opposition of rigid and curvilinear forms, is a synthesis that has nothing mechanical or vulgar about it. It suggests the structure of the genital organs and the dynamic of the sexual act. The same themes appear when

138 the complex is viewed from below: in the relationship between the porticoed walkways and the spatial cells of the classrooms, as well as in the key figure which drips water into a small fountain: shell, mouth, feminine figure *par excellence*. The architectural value of the school is certainly not a direct consequence of this symbolic content. It derives its value, rather, from the pure way in which content is translated into forms, using the specific means of architecture, with Porro's confidence in using the traditional masonry structure, filtered through the interpretive lens of modern architecture, in the complementary and dialectical use of the rational element (in the control of structure and technology) and of the emotional element, in the planning and linking of the images.

After the School for the Plastic Arts, Porro took up the theme of the assimilation of architecture with the living body: his most famous projects, the Palace of Air and Space, the House of Culture in Paris, a resort in Yugoslavia, a hotel complex in San Sebastian, treat the themes of his Cuban experiences, transposing them from a climate of faith and rational construction to one of uncertainty and nightmare, to a dramatic declaration of the end of hope. A grave family tragedy and a series of frustrations related to his teaching activity — caused by the difficulty in making his students of the Ècole des Beaux-Arts understand how much courage is necessary to exercise the power of the imagination — seem to have forced Porro to go from a joyful, open game to the "game of death," to a piteous exploration of the monstrous and abnormal. Regarding these dramatic and sorrowful developments in which, in Porro's words, "the sensitive expression of a great collective drama" is realized, the art center in Vaduz is a convincing escape, in which irony and hope coexist. The allusion to the capital of gold is ironic, realized in the golden crest crowning the building; the interior layout is full of positive implications, with its great terraces poised in the empty space enclosed by shining glass. From the outside, the golden rain is grasped by the fingers of a hand: once again the theme of the body reappears in an optimistic gesture of possession. It is fitting here to reread a passage from the

dialogue of Eupalinos by Paul Valéry, where the sense of the body is rediscovered by the mythical architect in the act of designing, when it seems to him that his body is part of the plan. "Grant me to find in thy alliance the feeling of what is true; temper, strenghten, and confirm my thoughts. Perishable as thou art, thou art far less so than my dreams" (translation by William McCausland Stewart, *Paul Valéry Dialogues*, New York, Pantheon Books, 1956).

In a world where the laws of the artificial world of industry tend to rob us of the direct sense of corporality, Porro's aspirations, hopes and delusions have some truth to them. They use architecture, this discipline that others would like to relegate to passively serve technology, giving up all cognitive efforts to enlighten the human condition.

Ricardo Bofill

Ricardo Bofill, El Taller de Arquitectura:
"Versailles pour le peuple,"
Saint-Quentin-en-Yvelines, 1980.

Ricardo Bofill, El Taller de Arquitectura:
Antigone residential complex, Montpellier,
1980, perspective of the central axis.

140 Ricardo Bofill is of Catalan and Italian origins, but has chosen France as his preferred place to experiment with his architectural ideas. He has succeeded in attracting the attention of the structures of a bureaucratic power as jealous as ever of its own national identity. Where Bernini failed three centuries ago when he was invited to design the expansion of the Louvre, Bofill has succeeded, in spite of some disappointments (Chirac's order to demolish the buildings, just being built, destined to close up the great hole of Les Halles) by virtue of his great capacity to speak with architecture in many languages, and with a perfect accent. There is no doubt, in fact, that in the Arcades du Lac, a residential complex already partially completed in the new town of St. Quentin, Bofill expresses himself "in French," bringing back to life that patrimony of urbanistic models of unsurpassable value that constitute the great French contribution to the European city, from the Place Royal to the Boulevard. Royal piazzas in a world in which power itself is questioned, and constitutes the symbolic counterpart of all intellectual work: what sense does it have? Is it right for the middle class to build its Versailles, and for grandeur to show up in the periphery? Bofill, like the majority of the most talented exponents of his generation, seems to be saying that the reconquest of "urbanity," of the city effect of the measured and welcoming character of space, of the simplicity and clarity of the urban structure, are well worthwhile, and justify every apparent and polemical anachronism. History proves that forms and models survive the type of power that produced them, and that their meaning changes in time according to the social use that is made of them. The Place des Vosges in Paris was created to affirm the prestige of an absolute power. But today, that closed square of houses surrounding a park, with those two-toned façades animated by brick and stone, evokes a sense of ordered cooperation, of civil cohabitation, of a more modern relationship, of a rare balance between nature and the city. This is certainly more acceptable to us than that schizophrenic and perverse relationship that characterizes the idiotic and caricatural futuristic prospecting of the

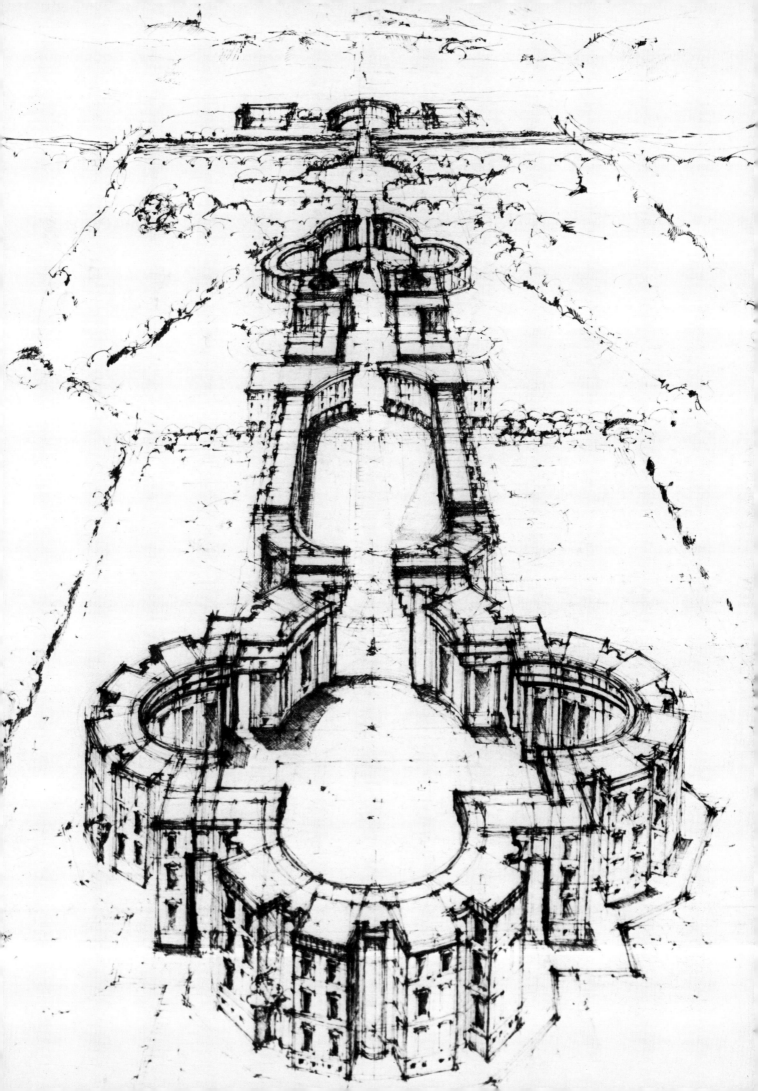

Ricardo Bofill, El Taller de Arquitectura:
*Antigone residential complex, Montpellier,
1980, elevation.*
Ricardo Bofill, El Taller de Arquitectura:
*Palacio de Abraxas, Marne-la-Vallée,
1979–1982, model.*

142

Defense quarter in Paris. Les Arcades du Lac use advanced methods of prefabrication, adopted even more convincingly by Bofill later on, and propose an urban grid of streets and piazzas cut at right angles. They rediscover the importance of the enclosed space that separates the city from nature, instead of dealing with it as in the urban periphery, arising from the distortion of the utopias of the Modern Movement, a continuation of natural chaos, a wild metaphor of a pre-social condition in the world. Nature enters into the city as a garden, reorganized on the scale of man, and architecture finds an agreement with it through the approved proportions of the humanistic tradition. That process of exchange and identification between the human body and the building is thus recreated, that profound sense of any classicism, that makes sense of the continual cyclical reflowering in history of this "infancy of the world."
In his most recent experiences, Bofill seems to demonstrate a paradox: that the industrialization of building — the construction by prefabricated parts, assembled in a rigorously programmed building site with the most advanced industrial methods — is not in conflict with the return of architecture to the wealth and linguistic complexity of classicism. On the contrary, it furthers this condition, and in a sense postulates it, for the exact need of regularity and easy individualization of parts that a similar techique makes necessary. The postmodern polemic, especially with Peter Blake's book *Form Follows Fiasco*, began trying to liquidate the idol of industrialization, often the cause of economic and constructive absurdities. The new wave of research into expression seemed anchored above all to the recovery of artisan techniques and traditional materials. Bofill has opposite ideas and is demonstrating his thesis in "three dimensions," realizing in Marne-la-Vallée and Montpellier two large residential complexes that greatly refine the methods and forms used in the "poor man's Versailles." In Marne-la-Vallée, in the immediate outskirts of Paris, the Palacio de Abraxas and the Theater, with its great apsidal profile, are almost complete, while the construction of the Antigone complex is about to begin in Montpellier.

These three works were designed one after the other, and demonstrate the development of Bofill's orientation. The Palacio is a very high block cut by empty spaces, into which light filters dramatically, as in an etching by Piranesi. The Theater has none of these mannerist contradictions. In its simple, superimposed parts, it reaches an extraordinary harmony of proportions deprived of any academic connotations by the faceted brilliance of glass columns reaching the full height of the building. Antigone weaves a well-balanced curtain around a large space, where rhythmic elements of the most distilled Renaissance repertoire are projected along with naturalistic elements. The result is surreal and oneiric, culminating in the innovative idea of the elements of the classical cornice interpreted as projecting balconies closing above the great apses.
Bofill's enemies say that the "grandeur" of his projects are better suited to the France of Giscard than to that of Mitterand, and they try to decode his symbolism as nostalgic and totalitarian. Besides the eloquent significance of his political past, and the battles fought against him by Chirac and the followers of Giscard — a building already under construction, part of his reorganization of Les Halles, was demolished after the commission was taken away from him — Bofill answers with facts. In Montpellier, the commission for the Antigone complex was awarded to him by the Socialist council which has usurped power for the first time from the traditionalist right, in power at least since the time of Richelieu. To these administrators aware of cultural facts (the mayor is an historian, the town planning commissioner an urban geographer), Bofill seemed to be the right one to give a "speaking" form to their renewal plan. Antigone will be their response to the Place Royal built by the central power in Paris to celebrate their victory over the Protestants which involved the massacre of a good part of the local bourgeoisie, the response to the fortress built by Richelieu to hold the city at bay and crush its rebellious instincts. With a ridiculous skyscraper and an enormous commercial center, the preceding city council had celebrated the splendor of consumerism, and had erected a curtain-wall city hall on a base inspired by

the forms of Richelieu's fortress. Bofill responds to the unconscious and woeful symbolism of the provincial followers of modernity with the transparent symbolism of collective spaces, protagonists of the city once again.

Christian de Portzamparc

Christian de Portzamparc: *project for a neighborhood in La Villette, 1977, axonometric projection.*

144 Speaking about his works in a lecture at the architecture school of the University of Milan, Christian de Portzamparc sang the praises of drawing. He demonstrated the importance of perspective in his working method which tends to reevaluate and rigorously control the optical and proportional aspects, and therefore to foresee the relationships among the parts of a completed building or among the parts of an urban whole. In addition he revealed how perspective was considered dated and was scorned during the years of his professional training; the only "modern" means was the axonometric projection that reproposes a mental and specialized knowledge of the architectural object. Portzamparc's latest work, already under construction, is the headquarters of a music conservatory connected to housing for the elderly. It is a typical expression of this "perspective" poetics, realizing not the simple and abstract planimetric combination of archetypal forms, but their connection and spatial penetration in the search of an effect that can be anticipated only by an elevation or by a model. The designed complex consists of the conservatory inserted in an isolated building and of the housing for the elderly, articulated in two blocks. One of these blocks is set back from the street, and serves as a background, developing the theme of perspective depth so dear to Renaissance architecture.

In the body of the conservatory, the temple colonnade of the ground floor and the tympanum of the roof are separate, kept apart by a harmonious play of volumes perforated with great courage in function of the interior spaces. The cylindrical stair calls attention to the process of decomposition and interference among the parts, creating a magical effect of bricolage, as in a painting by Savinio. Perhaps Portzamparc really wanted to express the complex freedom of music, because in his architecture, intervals, silences, and counterpoint become visible realities and not literary allusions.

Poet of the city in its contradictory and even chaotic essence, Portzamparc composes his buildings not as separate signed pieces lined up in the window of the space of the street, but as diverse and conflicting realities that reach a balance

Christian de Portzamparc: *project for a neighborhood in La Villette, 1977, perspective view.*

speaking about, showing and celebrating their diversity. The contrasts of scale and the large full surfaces that interrupt the continual vibration of the windows serve to exalt the specific quality of the urban scene, surprise, and narrative continuity. After the *Rue des Hautes-Formes*, the marvel of urban transplant was thus repeated: pieces of a new city caught in the middle of an anonymous periphery or, as in this case, in the old fabric of the city; pieces of the city, however, not decimated and sterile like the blocks of speculation or like the meteorites thrown about by the so-called moderns; but pieces of a living city endowed with that complexity or irreducibility to a mechanism proper to every biological reality.

Maurice Culot

Thanks to the work of a group of architects who joined together in the Atelier of Research and Urban Action (A.R.A.U.) headed by Maurice Culot, Brussels is becoming a reference point for the development of a new urban culture based on the abandonment of those cognitive and operative techniques that in the last fifty years have caused the sack of historic centers and the frightening chaos of the periphery. The Atelier gives neighborhood councils technical assistance, translated into alternative projects with respect to those proposed by private groups or by city authorities. In this way, opposition and protest are not expressed in the usual nonsense and utopia, but give rise to a concise criticism of the strategies of power. The A.R.A.U. fought its last battle with the defense committee of Saint-Gilles concerning the reconstruction of the Hotel des Monnaies, a nineteenth-century building bought by the city and razed to the ground to realize a good building program expressed through a sense of volumes that could only aggravate the damage produced in the city fabric. Culot's counterproposal substitutes the disorganized grouping of "boxes" in the modern style in the approved project, with a real square piazza, consciously inspired by the model of the Plaza Mayor in Madrid, surrounded by buildings typical of the city tradition. The difference of level in the borders of the space, which was resolved in the city project with blind scarp walls, is here used to animate the small piazza, creating within it spaces endowed with an identity and a warm relationship with its users, and enhanced by small pavilions: symbolic huts that repropose the most elementary of relationships and the richest mnemonic references between man and the enclosed space. Automobiles, which occupied a very visible place in the contested project, are gathered underground in the counter-project, leaving the piazza, often the site of a market, completely free to foot traffic. At least for the moment the town of Saint-Gilles seems determined to refuse the proposal of the neighborhood councils, and is holding fast to the approved project, entrusted to an architect of the same political party as the present administration. But the battle is raging, and an operation which could have been

translated into something positive for the city government is turning into an obvious error that could be reflected in the next elections.

It is significant that this time the basic fight is not limited to a request for services and "hygienic" requirements, but involves the form, the language and the cultural value of the intervention: it is a struggle for that quality that can surprise whoever thought that problems of architectural form are problems reserved for the experts, and that citizens must "let the architects be,"

respecting their autonomy and freedom, and permitting them, according to the poetics of the modern, to invent new "meteorites" each time to throw into the middle of the city.

The episode of the Hotel des Monnaies is typical of the battle between so-called modern culture, which by now is old and ready for the museum, and postmodern culture which, despite the violence and vulgarity of its enemies, continues to prosper and to influence young architects in every part of the world.

Maurice Culot and others: *reconstruction
of the area of the Hôtel des Monnaies,
Brussels, 1981, views.*

Livio Vacchini

148   For some years now, the canton of Ticino has once again become a reserve of architects, as in the time of Domenico Fontana, Maderno and Borromini. But instead of exporting these precious goods, as in the sixteenth and seventeenth-centuries (with tremendous advantage for Rome, the favorite destination of that migration), Ticino today has learned how to use it best, letting its most gifted architects realize buildings that are becoming one of the most important proofs of the great architectural changes of the late seventies. Besides Reinhardt, Reichlin and Mario Botta, Livio Vacchini deserves the most attention in this renaissance. His best works to date are two schools, one in Ai Saleggi (Locarno) and one in Losone, works in which the detachment from the functionalist method is more than evident, but takes place in a natural and bloodless way, without that store of paradoxes and gaudy decorative connotations that in other cases made the preservers of the modern lose control. The plans of the two schools are extremely clear, and enter that casuistry of classical typological solutions codified by J.M.L. Durand in his *Précis*, the bible of late neoclassicism, which has become fashionable in the last decade. Even the language behind the apparent call to rationalistic models of the twenties, hides an intentional recodification of forms through the mediation of architectural archetypes: the barrel vault, the portico, bilateral symmetry, the column, the play of proportions, the framed window and the use of continuous moldings that pick up the light and let the architecture describe itself, let it help the observer in recognizing the parts and their role in the unity of the work. This operation begins from the elementary nature of the forms suggested by technology to restore a further significance to them. It is easy to recognize in this operation a connection with collective memory, the reverse of that process of abstraction that led Mies van der Rohe, schooled in the tradition of Schinkel, to abandon the distilled classicism of his early works. The portico of the Locarno school has an iconic charge that comes from the tradition of the *gymnasion*, inseparable from the very idea of the school. The fact that small columns with capitals are

Livio Vacchini: *high school in Losone,*
general views and entrance.

substituted for the shapeless pilotis of the modern technological tradition expresses a desire for direct communication and a faith in the sound "pleasure" that sanctions the socialization that occurs in a work of architecture. In the school in Losone, the use of color and the complexity of the system of proportions add an unexpected tone of dialectal cordiality to the conceptual classical rigor; effects, impressions which are very unusual for an architecture that makes great use of non-traditional materials, an obvious sign of an uncommon capacity to completely change one's mind and to face some reasonable risks behind an apparent caution. When asked about his attitude toward tradition, Vacchini proved that he had no inhibitions: "The architect is always faced with the dilemma: resemblance or contrast? Contrast is an element of variety, but breaks one's attention. Resemblance, on the other hand, arises from a desire for unity. Architecture is art, and so it follows by definition that it is 'continuation.' Nothing exists outside tradition. Whatever is not tradition is plagiary."

Vacchini understands perfectly what makes the new architecture run: the renewal and restoration of the conventions that make communication possible inasmuch as they form the collective architectural code. "When I use a conventional language," Vacchini stated in *A+U*, "I do it so that everyone will understand me, and to escape from a culture of individualist intellectuals. I always do this with a touch of irony because I like dealing with the past in this way, laughing at my limits and ignorance. I devote particular attention to dialect. I live in a small town in the country, and my mother tongue is a dialect. How could I ignore it?... I have learned that every historical fact, whether recent or old, can be an incentive to reawaken our creative faculties."

The serenity inspired by this classicism on a human scale can astonish and alarm us, but it is a real fact translated into square meters of finished buildings.

Hans Robert Hiegel

In 1984 Berlin will host the largest architectural exhibition of all time: the Internationale Bauhausstellung Berlin (IBA). It will be a very unusual exhibition, similar in certain ways to the Weissenhof Kolonie built in Stuttgart in 1927 and to the Interbau of the sixties. It will not be a show of photographs and models, but an exhibition of realized buildings. While the Weissenhof was a small neighborhood of a few houses grouped on the slope of a hill, the IBA will be a piece of a city, or better, the reconstruction and expansion of one of the grandest and most glorious of all European cities, the old capital of Germany. The idea of the IBA comes, naturally, from West Berlin. Deprived of an adequate hinterland the city passed through a long period of crisis, and is still in search of a real heart since almost its entire historic center lies in East Berlin. The IBA plan for reconstruction, renewal and expansion regards zones within and outside of the urban nucleus, and in particular the area near the "wall" that separates the two cities. This zone has maintained more or less its look from the period immediately after the war, and the lacerations produced by pattern bombing are still visible in the urban fabric. Here, the most conspicuous and representative buildings will rise, awarded by the IBA through competitions to architects of the new generations who have firsthand experience in the problems of urban space and have abandoned the tradition of the Modern Movement.

Among the premiated projects in one of the competitions for the Friedrichstadt area, one work in particular deserves mention. It is a work by the German architect Hans Robert Hiegel, typical exponent of the tendency to rethink the city, making traditional archetypes reemerge within it, reinterpreted in light of a culture that has witnessed the separation between forms and meanings, a real eclipse of meaning. He is part of a tendency to view this devastation with a mixture of satisfaction and nostalgia for the strength of the ancient conventional codes. Hiegel's tower is above all a "tower," and tries to affirm its typical nature. To emphasize the entrance, the architect devised a sign both explicit and ambiguous: half Renaissance portal, simplified and corroded like a piece of

Hans Robert Hiegel: *project for the
reconstruction of a quarter in West Berlin,
1982, details.*

wood smoothed down by the movement of
waves, and half surveyor's stake, a stick
painted with stripes, similar to road signs.
The archetype of the tower, reinterpreted
through Ledoux, is the image to which
Hiegel pays homage, with an impassioned
candor that creates something both
disquieting and familiar: a typical example
of the products of recent architectural
culture, engaged in the search for a
recodification of the elements of urban
space.

Monta Mozuna

"An idea of mankind created cosmic
architecture that has evolved since the time
when 4,030,000,000 years ago, Amitabha
whose teachings are still with us today,
entered Nirvana. This architecture will
continue to evolve until the reincarnation of
Maitreya who will save mankind
46,070,000,000 years later.
Amitabha's deep meditation and Maitreya's
power of realization are manifested in the
materialization of the spirit, or essence: the
Energy of the ideation of the invisible
structures of the universe becomes the
worldly image in the columns that support
the Earth, a myriad of stars, the
planetary-earthly globe, the platform of the
world, the kingdom of the skies and a plan
of the starry heavens. It can therefore be
said that architecture possesses certain
mythological elements, like underground
streams, taken from the primitive Ocean of
the Earth: eruptions of the globe, the
attraction of the moon, solar combustion,
the planetary system, a knowledge of the
orientation of the stars."
Cosmology and esoteric inspiration have
taken hold even among architects, and
especially in Japan, where the figure of the
architect of the past few generations has
been divided schizophrenically between the
enticements of technology and the most
banal professionalism, and the allure of
"architectural magic:" an art requiring the
narcissist cult of one's own personality and
recourse to the imagination in each moment
of one's life and career. Even in this case it
is not difficult to understand the reasons
for certain choices in the transformations of
a society in which the science of
information has made tremendous
advances, while the encounter with Western
culture has produced an undefined process
of inexhaustible uprooting.
The more the elements of our civilization
are absorbed, the more antibodies are
developed that repropose the original
Oriental identity in new form.
Monta Mozuna has built several noteworthy
houses and an evocative Zen temple,
impeccably elegant, working with the
archetype of the hut emptied out and
enclosed in a homologous container that
echoes its structure. The use of light and
the observer's sense of estrangement give
life to a truly magical effect. "Naturally,
just as the image of the universe changes,

Monta Mozuna: *Zen Temple, Tokyo, 1979,
details of the interior.*

Monta Mozuna: *Allegorical drawing, 1980.* ▷

so does that of architecture," writes Monta
Mozuna. "There is hardly need to cite the
examples of the platonic universe of the
Renaissance, or the eliptical Baroque
universe. Leaving aside the question of
Utopia and Anti-Utopia, if Vitruvius, Plato,
Lao-tzu, Kukai, Alberti, Saint Ignatius, the

Genshin priests, Campanella, Garnier and
Le Corbusier felt the influence of
Amitabha's faculties of ideation and
Maitreya's power of realization on the brain
cells of mankind, there should be no need
to deny the same to Monta Mozuna,
megalomaniac architect."

It his self-definition as a megalomaniac,
Monta Mozuna plays an effective and very
up-to-date card, sublimating in self-irony a
need for the absolute, for metaphysical
certainties that resurface precisely where
the mechanism of progress seems to have
carried out its sterilizations most forcefully.

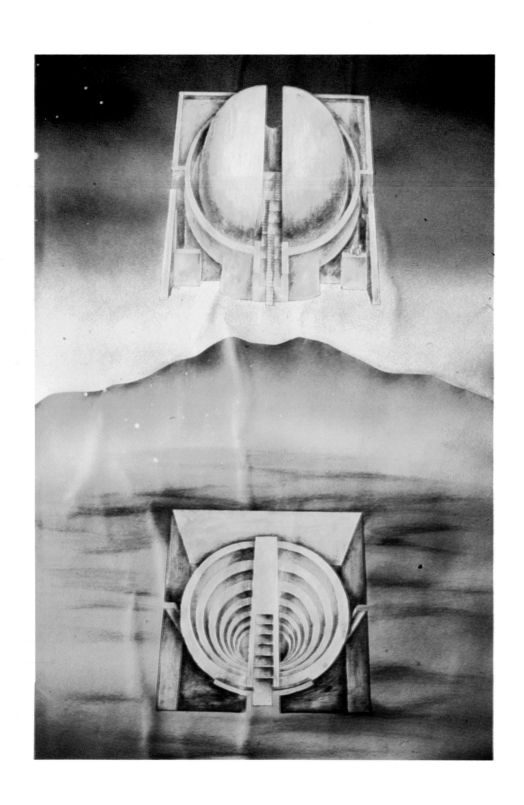

Our thanks to all those who kindly
contributed photographic material.
Among them:
Leo Castelli, New York; C. Bruce Forster,
Portland; Paolo Gasparini, Rome;
Giacomelli, Venice; Heinrich Helfenstein,
Zurich; HNK Architectural Photography,
Chicago; Osamu Murai, Tokyo; Richard
Payne, Houston; Julius Shulman, Los
Angeles; Serena Vergano, Barcelona.